W9-CAE-970

Benjamin Franklin

Scientist, Inventor, Printer, and Statesman

Leaders of the American Revolution

Leaders of the American Revolution

Benjamin Franklin
Scientist, Inventor, Printer, and Statesman

Hal Marcovitz

CHELSEA HOUSE
PUBLISHERS
An imprint of Infobase Publishing

Benjamin Franklin

Chelsea House
An imprint of Infobase Publishing
132 West 31st Street
New York NY 10001

Library of Congress Cataloging-in-Publication Data

Marcovitz, Hal.
  Benjamin Franklin: scientist, inventor, printer, and statesman/Hal Marcovitz.
    p. cm.—(Leaders of the American Revolution)
  Includes bibliographical references and index.
ISBN 0-7910-9219-4
  1. Franklin, Benjamin, 1706–1790—Juvenile literature. 2. Statesmen—United
States—Biography—Juvenile literature. 3. Inventors—United States—Biography—
Juvenile literature. 4. Scientists—United States—Biography—Juvenile literature.
5. Printers—United States—Biography—Juvenile literature. I. Title. II. Series.
E302.6.F8M33 2005
973.3092—dc22   2005031758

Chelsea House books are available at special discounts when purchased in bulk
quantities for businesses, associations, institutions, or sales promotions. Please call
our Special Sales Department in New York at (212) 967-8800 or (800) 322-8755.

You can find Chelsea House on the World Wide Web at http://www.chelseahouse.com

Series and cover design by Keith Trego

Printed in the United States of America

Bang 21C 10 9 8 7 6 5 4 3 2 1

This book is printed on acid-free paper.

All links, web addresses, and Internet search terms were checked and verified to be
correct at the time of publication. Because of the dynamic nature of the web, some
addresses and links may have changed since publication and may no longer be valid.

Author's Note
The letters and other writings of Benjamin Franklin frequently contain variant
spellings of words, capitalizations, and other types of usage that were common during
his time. Quotations taken from those writings included in this book have retained
these usages in order to preserve the flavor of the original writings.

Contents

"Doctor"
Benjamin Franklin

Just two months after the Declaration of Independence was signed in Philadelphia, the Continental Congress received word that leaders of the British military wished to hold informal peace talks with the Americans. In September 1776, three members of the Congress were dispatched to Staten Island, New York, for a meeting with British

Admiral Lord Richard Howe. The American emissaries were John Adams of Massachusetts, Edward Rutledge of South Carolina, and Benjamin Franklin of Pennsylvania.

Adams was suspicious of Howe's intentions, believing that the admiral had nefarious motives for asking for the peace conference. The other members of Congress were hopeful that peace could be arranged quickly, and a long and bloody war avoided. Adams was also hesitant to make the journey for other reasons. He was suffering from a cold at the time and hardly felt well enough to travel. In addition, Adams did not enjoy Franklin's company and did not relish the idea of spending two days on the road with Franklin, who was 30 years his senior and whom he regarded as pompous and self-centered. Franklin, Adams would write, had a "monopoly of reputation here and an indecency in displaying it."[1]

Nevertheless, Adams agreed to make the journey. On the morning of September 9, Rutledge and Franklin departed Philadelphia by coach while Adams rode alongside on horseback. The fresh air and sunshine improved Adams's spirits, but as the day wore on his cold symptoms flared up. To make matters worse, when

Franklin, Adams, and Rutledge arrived in New Brunswick, New Jersey, to spend the night, they found the inn quite crowded, with only modest accommodations available. In fact, Franklin and Adams learned they had to share not only a tiny room, but the room's single bed as well.

As the two men prepared for bed, Adams shut the room's single window. "Oh!" said Franklin. "Don't shut the window. We shall be suffocated."[2] Adams responded that he suffered from a cold and feared the cool night air, but Franklin dismissed his complaint.

"The air within this chamber will soon be, and is indeed now, worse than that outdoors," Franklin told Adams. "Come! Open the window and come to bed, and I will convince you. I believe you are not acquainted with my theory of colds."[3]

Franklin had, in fact, made quite a study of the common cold. He concluded that colds were caused not by chilly breezes, but by germs passed from human to human through sneezes, coughs, kisses, and other occasions in which people manage to breathe on one another. "Traveling in our severe winters, I have often suffered cold sometimes to the extremity only short of freezing, but this did not make me catch cold," Franklin wrote in a letter to his friend Dr. Benjamin Rush. "People often catch cold from one another when shut up together in close rooms, coaches, etc., and when sitting near and conversing so as to breathe in each others transpiration."[4] Indeed, Franklin had come to that conclusion in 1773—a century before French microbiologist Louis Pasteur's theories on infectious germs gained widespread acceptance.

EXERCISE AND AIR BATHS

As his ideas on the common cold would suggest, Franklin was fascinated with medicine. He developed many theories that proved he knew more about the workings of the human body than many of the most prominent physicians of the era. Although Franklin had received an honorary doctor-of-laws degree from a Scottish university, he was by no means a practicing doctor of medicine—in fact, he left school as a young boy to learn the printer's trade.

Nevertheless, Franklin was convinced, for example, that exercise helped improve health. An avid swimmer his whole life, Franklin studied how people exercised and observed how body temperature rose while people exerted themselves. His experiments showed that

In September 1776, three members of the Continental
Congress—John Adams, Edward Rutledge, and Benjamin
Franklin—agreed to meet with British Admiral Lord Richard
Howe on Staten Island, in hopes of reaching a peace
agreement that would end the revolution. Negotiations
failed, however, and the war for American independence
continued.

walking a mile up and down stairs produced five times more body warmth than simply walking a mile on a flat surface. He measured his own pulse rate while lifting heavy weights and deduced that his body temperature rose as his heart worked harder. Today, of course, it is a well-known fact that bodies burn calories—units of heat—during exercise. Franklin's experiments, however, were among the first conducted on the relationship between health and exercise.

Franklin was also first to recognize the dangers of lead poisoning. In print shops of the era, lead was heated and liquefied so it could be poured into molds to form characters of the alphabet. Franklin observed that printers who handled hot lead often suffered from stiffness and even paralysis—a malady known then as the "dry gripes." He also learned that people who consumed rum made in stills fashioned from lead coils suffered similar symptoms. He wondered whether there was something in the lead that made people ill, and urged rum makers to fashion their stills from tin. He wrote, "It affects among tradesmen those that use lead, however different their trades, as glazers, type-founders, plumbers, potters, white-lead makers and painters."[5] Lead-based products, such as paint and

In Benjamin Franklin's youth, there were no hospitals in America. In 1751, Franklin convinced the Pennsylvania Assembly to provide half of the financing needed to establish Pennsylvania Hospital, the first general hospital in the colonies. He raised the remaining funds from local businesses and residents. Pennsylvania Hospital, shown in this illustration, remains a thriving healthcare institution today.

gasoline, have since been outlawed, and industries that employ lead in their manufacturing processes must take precautions to shield workers from dangerous fumes.

Franklin realized the importance of hospitalizing sick people. In colonial America, there were no hospitals and those who were ill had to be treated at home. In 1751, he convinced the Pennsylvania Assembly to finance half the cost for Pennsylvania Hospital, the first medical institution to be erected in the colonies. He raised the other half of the money by obtaining donations from city businesses and residents. He also designed a thin, flexible metal tube that helped enhance the flow of urine in people who suffered from blocked urinary tracts—the forerunner of the modern catheter that is used today in hospitals everywhere. His brother John was the first patient to use the tube.

Franklin's experiments with electricity led him to believe that a mild electrical shock could cure palsy, body tremors that stem from a number of causes ranging from disease to genetic factors. Eventually, Franklin concluded that he "never knew any advantage from electricity in palsies that was permanent."[6] But he did recommend using electrical shocks as a treatment for "mad people"[7] and, years later, electroshock therapy became a common method for treating mental illness.

Sometimes, Franklin's ideas about medicine were not valid. He believed, for example, that human health could be enhanced by exposing the body to fresh air, so each morning, for no less than an hour, he would sit naked in front of an open window for what he called an "air bath."[8]

FIGHTING SMALLPOX

One of Franklin's greatest contributions to medicine did not involve an invention or discovery of his own, but his acceptance of the practice of vaccination to prevent the spread of disease. By the eighteenth century, smallpox was a particularly devastating disease. The virus often killed its victims; those who survived were usually left with ugly and disfiguring scars and pockmarks on their faces and other parts of their bodies. Physicians had concluded, though, that people could be inoculated against smallpox if they were exposed to a very tiny dose of the virus. To provide the vaccination, a doctor scraped the blister of a smallpox sufferer, withdrawing a tiny amount of fluid. Next, the doctor dipped a sharp knife into the smallpox blister fluid, and used the knife to scratch the skin of a healthy person, thus transferring a tiny dose of the disease. In some cases, the person receiving the vaccination contracted smallpox, but in most cases the patients did not develop symptoms. Later, physicians learned that a vaccination containing a similar disease, known as cowpox, was highly effective in preventing smallpox and usually resulted in no ill effects for the recipients.

Franklin fully embraced the concept of vaccination and urged the readers of his newspaper, the *Pennsylvania Gazette*, to have themselves inoculated against smallpox. Ironically, Franklin's second son, Francis Folger Franklin, died of smallpox in 1736 at the age of four. Franklin and his wife, Deborah, were devastated by the loss of their boy, whom they called "Franky." Franklin had intended to have the boy inoculated, but decided to wait until Franky recovered from a case of diarrhea. In the meantime, Franky contracted smallpox and died.

Soon after the boy's death, rumors circulated throughout Philadelphia that Franky had died from a smallpox vaccination. Franklin felt it necessary to set the record straight, so a week after the boy's death he reported the circumstances of Franky's death in the *Pennsylvania Gazette*: "I do hereby sincerely declare that he was not inoculated, but received the distemper in the common way of infection."[9]

He concluded by urging his readers to seek smallpox vaccinations. For the rest of his life, though, he mourned the loss of his son. Years later, when a sister wrote to him from London announcing the birth of a grandson, Franklin replied that the news brought "afresh to my mind the idea of my son Franky, though now dead thirty-six years, whom I have seldom since seen equaled in everything, and whom to this day I cannot think of without a sigh."[10]

A LENGTHY HARANGUE

As for how things turned out that night at the inn in New Brunswick, one person not willing to accept Franklin's theory about the common cold was John Adams. Standing in his nightshirt, the future president of the United States protested that, while he was familiar with Franklin's theory on the spread of colds, he chose to believe that a breath of chilly night air was likely to do him more harm than good. Rather than argue with Franklin, though, Adams left the window open, hopped quickly into bed, and he covered himself against the night breeze.

Franklin settled into bed as well, but before retiring for the night he insisted on reminding Adams of his theory about cold germs. Recalled Adams, "The Doctor then began a harangue, upon air and cold and respiration and perspiration, with which I was so much amused that I soon fell asleep, and left him and his philosophy together."[11]

The next morning, Franklin was pleased to report to Adams that he had not caught his fellow traveler's cold and insisted that the well-ventilated room carried the germs out the window. Eventually, Adams changed his opinion of Franklin and admired the older man's intelligence and craftiness. As for the meeting with Lord Howe, the three Americans declined to accept Howe's terms for peace and the revolution continued.

Test Your Knowledge

I Why did John Adams not wish to accompany Benjamin Franklin to peace talks with British General Howe at Staten Island?

  a. Adams was suspicious of Howe's motives.

  b. Adams was suffering from a cold.

  c. Adams disliked Franklin, finding him pompous and self-centered.

  d. All of the above.

2 Why did Franklin suggest that Adams leave the window of their room open?

  a. Franklin wanted Adams to get sicker.

  b. Franklin suspected that colds were spread by germs and not caused by cold air as people then thought.

  c. Franklin was hoping British raiders would kidnap Adams.

  d. Franklin was hoping to escape in the night and deliver a message to the British.

3 Although trained as a printer, Franklin loved science and contributed greatly to the study of

  a. medicine.

  b. astronomy.

  c. geology.

  d. ichthyology.

4 How did Franklin influence our ideas about illness and its treatment?

    a. He recognized that lead could be poisonous to those who handled it regularly.

    b. He suggested that the state found hospitals where the sick could receive consistent care.

    c. He embraced the idea of vaccination and encouraged others to do so.

    d. All of the above.

5 What was the outcome of the peace talks between Franklin, Adams, Rutledge, and Howe?

    a. The colonists accepted Howe's terms, but the British later broke the treaty.

    b. Rutledge was taken hostage while Adams and Franklin fled.

    c. The colonists rejected Howe's proposal, making war inevitable.

    d. None of the above.

ANSWERS: 1. d; 2. b; 3. a; 4. d; 5. c

Student and Apprentice

When Benjamin Franklin was a boy in Boston, Massachusetts, he discovered a love for swimming. He took naturally to the water, teaching himself and his friends how to swim. One day, he wandered down to the banks of Mill Pond and lofted a kite overhead. In the years ahead, Franklin would cement his place in the history of science by flying a kite and a key in a thunderstorm, but on this sunny summer day, young Benjamin had nothing more in mind than a leisurely afternoon of play.

As he watched the kite soar into the sky, he was struck with a curious thought: With the kite acting as a sail, could it pull a floating person across the pond? He quickly shed his clothes and, grasping the stick holding the kite string, waded into the pond and leaned back, letting himself float freely. As the wind caught the kite, he felt the unmistakable sensation of being towed across the pond. "Having then engaged another boy to carry my clothes round the pond," he later wrote, "I began to cross the pond with my kite, which carried me quite over without the least fatigue and with the greatest pleasure imaginable."[12]

Benjamin Franklin's love for the water did not stop with this single experiment with a kite. Still searching for a way to propel himself swiftly through the water, he concluded that the amount of water a swimmer could move with his hands and feet had a lot to do with how fast the swimmer could travel. So in 1717, at the age of 11, Benjamin used wooden slats to fashion a crude set of swim fins. He first devised them to fit over his hands, but when he found his wrists growing tired, he altered the design so he could wear them on the soles of his feet. The fins seemed to work, but Franklin later admitted they weren't designed very well. "I was not satisfied with them," he said, "because I observed that the stroke is partly given by the inside of the feet and the an[k]les, and not entirely with the soles of the feet."[13]

Nevertheless, throughout his life Franklin maintained a love for swimming and rarely passed up an opportunity to enjoy a dip in an invitingly cool river or pond. In fact, Franklin's devotion to the sport would later be recognized by the International Swimming Hall of Fame—he is the only signer of the Declaration of Independence to be so enshrined, having won his place among the sport's major stars in 1968.

FRANKLIN FAMILY ORIGINS

The Franklin family's roots can be traced to the village of Ecton, near Northampton, England, where Benjamin's great-great-grandfather, Thomas Francklyne, was born around 1540. Benjamin Franklin's father, Josiah, worked as a silk and cloth dyer, but had trouble making ends meet for his young family, which included his wife, Anne, and three young children. In 1683, Josiah and his family set sail for America, where he had heard the wages were higher and opportunities endless. Josiah and his wife settled in Boston, where Josiah took up the trade of "tallow chandler"—rendering animal fat into candles and soap. Josiah and Anne Franklin prospered in the New World and their family grew to include seven children, but in 1689 Anne died of illness.

Later that year, Josiah married a new wife, Abiah Folger. Josiah's already large family would continue to grow. Josiah and Abiah raised a total of ten children. Their eighth child was Benjamin Franklin, born on January 17, 1706, in the tiny Franklin family home on Milk Street in Boston.

Benjamin's father recognized his son's intelligence and magnetic personality early and initially planned a career in the ministry for his son. He hoped Benjamin would enroll in Harvard College and, to prepare him, he sent the boy, at the age of eight, to prestigious Boston Latin School. Young Benjamin was clearly the brightest boy in school, but after only a year Josiah suddenly withdrew his son from classes. Later, Franklin suggested that his father ran out of money, but historians have wondered whether Josiah Franklin convinced himself that Benjamin was not cut out for

Benjamin Franklin's beginnings were indeed humble. He was the eighth of ten children raised by his father Josiah and Josiah's second wife, Abiah Folger, in this house on Milk Street in Boston, Massachusetts. Josiah also had seven children with his first wife, Anne Child, before she died.

the ministry. The boy was inquisitive and prone to ask too many questions. He was also a jokester—hardly the type of personality one found among the ranks of the Puritan clergy.

One incident stands out in Franklin's youth: He and his playmates enjoyed fishing for minnows in a marshy area of Mill Pond. Often, the boys found themselves sinking into the mud as they fished. Franklin came up with the idea of building a wharf on which they could stand. To erect the wharf, they stole large stones intended for a new house. Franklin was clearly the ringleader. When their thievery was discovered, they were made to replace the stones. In his autobiography, Franklin recalled "several of us were corrected by our Fathers; and tho' I pleaded the Usefulness of the Work, mine convinc'd me that nothing was useful which was not honest."[14]

MAGICALLY MAGICAL SQUARES

Instead of planning for a career in the ministry, young Franklin took classes in writing and mathematics from neighborhood schoolmaster George Brownell. He excelled in writing but failed mathematics. Nevertheless, even with his abysmal record in mathematics, Franklin is given credit for devising, as a young boy, a mathematical puzzle known as "magic squares" that has stumped mathematicians for three centuries. He later wrote to his friend Peter Collinson,

In my younger days, having once some leisure which I still think I might have employed more usefully, I had amused myself in making these kind of magic squares, and at length had acquired such a knack at it that I could fill the cells of any magic square, of reasonable size, with a series of numbers as fast as I could write them, disposed in such a manner as that the sums of every row, horizontal, perpendicular, or diagonal, should be equal.[15]

In fact, he was able to craft rows of numbers, which had seemingly been chosen at random, but when added resulted in equal sums, regardless of whether they were totaled across, up and down, or with some diagonal variation. His magic square of eight rows, for example, totals 260 no matter how it is added (*see box on page 22*).

His masterpiece, though, was the magic square he concocted with 16 rows of numbers, which totaled 2,056 regardless of how they were added. Over the centuries, many mathematicians have wrestled with the question of how Franklin constructed the rows. Some mathematicians have proposed complicated algebraic formulas, but they are also quick to point out that the young boy who failed mathematics in George Brownell's classroom is hardly likely to have been capable of devising an equation that would have

52	61	4	13	20	29	36	45
14	3	62	51	46	35	30	19
53	60	5	12	21	28	37	44
11	6	59	54	43	38	27	22
55	58	7	10	23	26	39	42
9	8	57	56	41	40	25	24
50	63	2	15	18	31	34	47
16	1	64	49	48	33	32	17

This magic square totals 260 whether the numbers are added horizontally or vertically.

established which numbers fit properly into each place in the puzzle. Most mathematicians have concluded that Franklin probably constructed the puzzle through tedious trial and error. Author and mathematician Jim Moran wrote of Franklin:

Ben has always been one of my idols, and now he has gone and tarnished his image and revealed to me as being merely human. In telling his colleague Collinson that he could make his magic squares as fast as he could write down the numbers, he was pushing reasonable exaggeration beyond the limit. I just can't buy this, and I say nobody but *nobody* can perform this feat. He even claimed to do this with squares of any reasonable size. *No way!*[16]

As for Franklin, he never revealed the truth behind the construction of his magic squares and only had this to say about the secret behind his magic square of 16: "You will readily allow this square of 16 to be the most magically magical of any magic square ever made by any magician."[17]

"A TOLERABLE ENGLISH WRITER"

After a year of study under Brownell, Franklin dropped out to take up the candle and soap trade. His two years of schooling—one at Boston Latin and one under Brownell—would be the only two years of formal education Franklin received in his lifetime.

Franklin also lasted just a short time in his father's shop; he hated working among the boiling cauldrons of animal fat and disclosed to his father that he was harboring the notion of finding work as a merchant seaman. Josiah Franklin discouraged Benjamin's adventurous nature—one of his sons, Josiah Jr., had been lost at sea—and instead the two searched for a trade that Benjamin might find more to his liking. He first tried cutlery, working a few days for a cousin in a knife-making business, but when the cousin demanded a stiff apprenticeship fee from Josiah, Benjamin was sent instead to learn the printing trade from his older brother, James.

So began a testy relationship with his brother that would last for the next six years. By day, Franklin learned the printer's trade—the techniques of fashioning and setting type. At night, he filled his hours reading and honing his writing style. There was, indeed, plenty of business in James Franklin's print shop, which produced the *New-England Courant*, an upstart weekly newspaper founded by James to challenge Boston's two established papers, the *Boston Gazette* and *Boston News-Letter*.

From the start, the *Courant* struggled to survive. The two established newspapers enjoyed the support of the colonial government and, therefore, did not have to pay heavy postage fees to ship copies through the mail. The *Courant*, however, had to rely on its content to sell papers, making use of snappy writing, wry commentary, and biting satire. James Franklin modeled the *Courant* after *The Spectator*, the well-read London journal of commentary and witty prose.

James Franklin's print shop became a gathering place for a youthful literary community that was taking root in Boston. Young writers gathered at the *Courant* offices to praise and criticize the prose they read in James Franklin's newspaper. James Franklin's young apprentice undoubtedly listened in on their conversations as he toted trays of heavy type, anxious to one day join their crowd. "Hearing their conversations, and their accounts of the approbation their papers were received with, I was excited to try my hand among them," he wrote.[18]

Franklin knew that his own talent as a writer needed polishing. To become a writer, he would first have to become an accomplished reader. Franklin immersed himself in whatever books he could find. Josiah Franklin owned a small collection of books, and Benjamin read every volume on his father's shelves. He was greatly impressed with *Bonifacius: Essays to*

Do Good, by Cotton Mather, the Puritan leader of Boston. The book instilled in him a sense of responsibility toward his community. Years later, Franklin wrote to Mather's son, "If I have been a useful citizen, the public owes the advantage of it to that book."[19]

He soon exhausted his father's collection and found himself searching for other books. In Boston during the early eighteenth century, books were quite hard to come by, particularly for an apprentice with little spending money. Books were expensive and most of them had to be imported from Great Britain and other European countries because American print shops produced few book-length works. Libraries were virtually unheard of.

Whenever he did find a new book, he was always anxious to share it with his friend, John Collins, whom Franklin called "another bookish lad."[20] The two boys would both read the same book, then talk about the lessons they learned. Soon, they agreed to stage debates on the merits of the books. In the eighteenth century, the art of oration was a much-valued skill. The era's most learned scholars and statesmen were admired for their ability to think on their feet and make their points in public forums. Debating against

John Collins, Benjamin Franklin learned that he could be much more effective by using gentle and persuasive arguments than by employing a direct and confrontational attack. According to Franklin, being "disputatious" is a "very bad habit."[21]

When Franklin came across several copies of *The Spectator*, he soaked up every word. He honed his writing style by reading *The Spectator's* essays, taking notes, and then trying his hand at rewriting the essays in his own words. He even turned some of *The Spectator* essays into poems, thinking the technique would help improve his vocabulary because he would have to search for just the right words to fit into his lines of verse. Then, he took the poems and turned them back into essays. This constant act of writing and rewriting helped Franklin develop his craft as a writer. Franklin later concluded,

I sometimes had the pleasure of fancying that in certain particulars of small import I had been lucky enough to improve the method or the language, and this encouraged me to think that I might possibly in time come to be a tolerable English writer, of which I was extremely ambitious."[22]

(continued on page 30)

Benjamin Franklin, a Very Bad Poet

The lighthouse at the entrance to Boston Harbor is known as Boston Light; it is the second oldest lighthouse in America, preceded only by Sandy Hook Light in New Jersey. Boston Light was erected on Beacon Island in 1716 and rebuilt in 1783 after it was destroyed during the American Revolution. In 1718, the lighthouse keeper, George Worthylake, his wife Ann, daughter Ruth, a slave named Shadwell, and Worthylake's friend, John Edge, mysteriously drowned as they headed to Beacon Island in a canoe.

The story inspired Benjamin Franklin to write a poem titled "The Lighthouse Tragedy." At the time, Franklin worked as an apprentice in his brother's print shop. James Franklin was so impressed with the poem that he published it in a pamphlet, which Benjamin then peddled on the streets of Boston, earning a few shillings for his effort. Reprinted in 1959 in the first volume of *The Papers of Benjamin Franklin*, the poem begins:

> *Oh! George, This wild November*
> *We must not pass with you*
> *For Ruth, our fragile daughter,*
> *It's chilly gales will rue*

Encouraged by the success of "The Lighthouse Tragedy," Franklin soon wrote a second poem, which

his brother published as well. The poem told the story of the notorious pirate Edward Teach, also known as Blackbeard. Reprinted in the 2003 book *Ben Franklin's Almanac*, "A Sailor's Song on the Taking of Teach or Blackbeard the Pirate," begins:

> *Will you hear of a bloody battle,*
> *Lately fought upon the seas,*
> *It will make your ears to rattle,*
> *And your admiration cease:*
> *Have you heard of Teach the Rover,*
> *And his knavery on the Main;*
> *How of gold he was a lover,*
> *How he loved ill got gain.*

Alas, Franklin's career as a poet appears to have ended following the publication of his pirate poem. In his autobiography, Franklin admitted that his poems were "wretched Stuff," and although he did make a little money by peddling them on Boston streets, his father "discourg'd me, by ridiculing my Performances, and telling me Verse-makers were generally Beggars; so I escap'd being a Poet, most probably a very bad one."

(continued from page 27)

SILENCE DOGOOD

He would soon get his chance. At the age of 16, Franklin composed a series of essays written under the pen name "Silence Dogood," supposedly an aging, prudish widow whose advice and sage observations on life were laced with generous doses of humor, irony, and biting sarcasm. By that time, Franklin's relationship with his brother had grown strained. James was jealous of his brother. He mistreated him at the print shop and occasionally struck his young apprentice. Franklin was well aware that his brother would never permit him to publish a word in the *Courant*, so he devised a strategy to submit the essays anonymously. Disguising his handwriting, he composed the first essay and slipped it under the print shop door late one night. The next morning, the group of young Boston writers and literary critics discovered it and immediately saw its merits. On April 2, 1722, the essay was published on the front page of the *Courant*.

The 14 Silence Dogood essays published between April and October 1722 are the first examples of what has become a popular and enduring form of humor in America: wry, homespun stories, told in an innocent and naïve voice, that poke fun at all levels of American

This mural by Charles Mills shows a glimpse of Benjamin Franklin's early years at work in his brother's print shop. It was during this time that Franklin not only learned the printer's trade, but also honed his skills as a writer and satirist.

life. Humorists such as Mark Twain in the nineteenth century, Will Rogers in the twentieth century, and Garrison Keillor in the twenty-first century owe a great debt to Silence Dogood.

Franklin aimed the Silence Dogood essays at many targets. The students at Harvard College—where many of his former Boston Latin School classmates were now attending—"were little better than Dunces and Blockheads." To the drunkards of Boston, whom Franklin believed to be far too many in number, he had Mrs. Dogood observe that while a man never admits he is drunk, he will agree that he is "boozey, tipsey, fox'd, mellow, feaverish, almost froze, in his altitudes, sees two moons, &c."[24]

Through Mrs. Dogood, Franklin became one of America's earliest proponents for the education of women, regarded then as an outlandish idea. He wrote,

> One would wonder how it should be that Women are conversible at all, since they are only beholding to natural Parts for all their Knowledge. Their Youth is spent to teach them to stitch and sew, or make Baubles: They are taught to read indeed, and perhaps to write their Names, or so; and that is the Heighth of a Womans Education.[25]

Through Mrs. Dogood, Franklin declared several ideas that would find their way into the U.S. Constitution nearly three-quarters of a century later. In one case, Mrs. Dogood stood up for freedom of speech—which was hardly a right universally enjoyed under the reign of the English king:

> Without Freedom of Thought, there can be no such Thing as Wisdom; and no such Thing as Publick

This etching shows a young Benjamin Franklin, at work as a printer, as he overhears praise for his first essay. Franklin's talents as a writer would also serve him well as a journalist, scientist, and statesman.

Liberty, without Freedom of Speech; which is the Right of every Man, as far as by it, he does not hurt or controul the Right of another: And this is the only Check it ought to suffer, and the only Bounds it ought to know.

This sacred Privilege is so essential to free Governments that the Security of Property, and the Freedom of Speech always go together; and in those wretched Countries where a Man cannot call his Tongue his own, he can scarce call any Thing else his own. Whoever would overthrow the Liberty of a Nation, must begin by subduing the Freeness of Speech; a Thing terrible to Publick Traytors.[26]

The Silence Dogood essays were immensely popular among the *Courant*'s readers. Meanwhile, though, Franklin's relationship with his brother continued to worsen. After the fourteenth essay was published, Franklin found himself out of ideas. So, he disclosed to his brother that he was, in fact, the author of the Silence Dogood essays. The vain and jealous James Franklin reacted with anger, believing a joke had been played on him. With James now openly hostile to him, Franklin decided to quit his apprenticeship. Franklin bought passage aboard a ship bound for New York and, on September 25, 1723, he slipped quietly aboard and departed Boston, "a Boy of but 17, without the least Recommendation to or Knowledge of any Person in the Place, and with very little Money in my Pocket."[27]

Test Your Knowledge

I Why is Franklin recognized by the International Swimming Hall of Fame?

   a. He invented the butterfly stroke.

   b. As a young man, he set a speed swimming record that held for a century.

   c. He was devoted to swimming as both sport and recreation, and even designed an early set of swim fins.

   d. None of the above.

2 Franklin's father, Josiah, hoped that the young Benjamin would become

   a. a scientist.

   b. a minister.

   c. a statesman.

   d. a soldier.

3 What were Franklin's "magic squares"?

   a. A way of calculating the distance to the stars

   b. A way of predicting the weather

   c. A puzzle in which the numbers in any row, whether vertically, horizontally, or diagonally, add to the same sum

   d. None of the above

4 How did the young Franklin spend his free time while employed at his brother's newspaper?

     a. Franklin became an avid reader, devouring any book he could find.

     b. Franklin daydreamed of becoming a minister.

     c. Franklin designed new and better printing machines for his brother.

     d. None of the above.

5 Who was Silence Dogood?

     a. A rich widow and an early sponsor of James Franklin's newspaper, the *Courant*

     b. A pen name used by Franklin to get his columns published in the *Courant*

     c. A colonist who opposed Franklin's bold advocacy of free speech

     d. None of the above

ANSWERS: 1. c; 2. b; 3. c; 4. a; 5. b

Printer and Journalist

Benjamin Franklin was able to raise money for his passage aboard ship by selling his books. He had many books to sell because, while apprenticing for his brother James, Franklin found he could save money to buy those books if he stuck to a strict vegetarian diet.

Franklin stayed briefly in New York. Today, New York City is a bustling metropolis and, with some 8 million people, it is the largest city in the United States. When Benjamin Franklin stepped off the boat in 1723, however, New York was a small town—much smaller than Boston. In fact, New York had only one newspaper and one print shop, and when Franklin called on William Bradford, the print-shop proprietor, he learned that Bradford had no job to offer. But Bradford's son, Andrew, ran a print shop in Philadelphia and he might need an experienced printer. Franklin made the 90-mile journey south by foot and boat, and ten days after leaving Boston, he set foot in Philadelphia, the city that would serve as his hometown for the next 67 years.

Stepping onto the busy cobblestone streets for the first time, Franklin was dazzled and quite lost in all the activity. He spent the last of his money on "three puffy rolls," eating one and giving the others to a mother and daughter whom he had met on the boat coming down from New York. He spent time wandering the streets, finally making his way to the print shop of Andrew Bradford.

This sketch by Edward Penfield shows a young Benjamin Franklin walking along a Philadelphia street during his first visit to the city in 1723. Franklin would soon make Philadelphia his home, later publishing both the *Pennsylvania Gazette* and *Poor Richard's Almanac*.

Franklin worked for Bradford for only a short while before he found employment in a print shop owned by Samuel Keimer. His new employer was elderly and eccentric, and his printing equipment was old and worn out. But Franklin was delighted to be living on his own. He was free from his brother's jealousy, and as a journeyman, or professional, printer, he was able to earn more money than the meager apprentice wages that James was willing to pay. What's more, Keimer helped Franklin find lodgings in the home of a friend, John Read, where Franklin made the acquaintance of Read's daughter, Deborah. A romance would soon blossom.

While living with the Reads, Franklin received a letter from a brother-in-law, Robert Holmes, who said that Franklin's family back in Boston was concerned about how Benjamin was doing on his own in Philadelphia. Franklin wrote back, explaining that he was getting along very nicely on his own and that he had a fine job in a busy print shop. Holmes showed Franklin's reply to his friend, Sir William Keith, the colonial governor of Pennsylvania, who was immediately impressed with the eloquence of the teenage boy's letter. The next time Keith was in Philadelphia, he called on Franklin and, after speaking with Benjamin over a glass of wine, declared that he would help set up young Franklin in his own printing business. Keith urged Franklin to go to England to buy a printing press and other equipment he needed and said that he would guarantee Franklin's credit, meaning the governor promised to pay whatever debts Franklin incurred.

PENNILESS TIMES

Franklin left for England in November 1724. He was 18 then and had been living on his own in Philadelphia for a year. He arrived in London on Christmas Eve and soon discovered that despite Keith's position and title in America, the colonial governor was broke and in no position to guarantee anyone's credit. Nearly penniless, Franklin found a place to stay and a job in a London print shop.

Franklin spent two years in London, working as a printer, making many friends, and developing a love for the city and an appreciation for English culture, which would help make him an effective diplomat years later when he returned to London as a representative of the colonies. While living in London, he gave swimming lessons and, when some friends suggested that he establish his own swimming school, Franklin sought the advice of fellow Philadelphian Thomas Denham.

Denham was a merchant whom Franklin had met on the trip over. Denham advised Franklin that a swimming school was probably not a good idea, and instead offered Franklin a job. If he would return to Philadelphia, Denham would place him in charge of a general store that he planned to open in the city.

Franklin accepted the offer, and in the summer of 1726 the two men boarded a ship home.

Unfortunately, the job in Denham's store lasted just a few months. Denham died soon after the two men returned to Philadelphia and the store was closed. Once again, Franklin found himself virtually penniless. Reluctantly, he went back to work for Keimer.

While working for Keimer, though, Franklin helped revolutionize the printing industry in America. At the time, printers produced books, newspapers, pamphlets, and other materials using the process known as "letter-press." The letterpress process involved composing a "bank" of English letters of the alphabet that had been cast individually in lead, applying a layer of ink, then pressing sheets of paper onto the bank to create the printed pages.

The process of casting the letters in lead had to take place in a foundry where molds were created. At the foundry, the lead was heated into liquid form and then poured into the molds. At the time, there were no foundries in America capable of producing the lead letters. There were also no "typeface" designers in America. In printing, the typeface is a particular style of letters. Some typefaces are bold, some are thin, some are designed with fancy curves and curlicues, and some are quite simple.

When Franklin returned to America and went back to work for Keimer, all printers in the colonies had to obtain their typefaces from England or other European countries. It was expensive, to be sure, and Keimer could ill-afford to replace his old and worn out type-faces with new styles shipped from across the ocean. So, Franklin used Keimer's old typefaces to create new molds, thus becoming the first printer in America to manufacture type. In 1902, renowned typeface designer Morris Fuller Benton created a style of type he called Franklin Gothic, to honor Benjamin Franklin's ground-breaking work in American typography.

PENNSYLVANIA GAZETTE

Franklin didn't stay long in Keimer's shop. In 1728, he struck up a partnership with Keimer's apprentice Hugh Meredith, whose father was willing to put up the money to start them in business on their own. The partnership of Franklin and Meredith was immediately successful, thanks mostly to Franklin's hard work and cleverness in attracting business. As for Meredith, he drank too much. Within a year, Franklin found some friends willing to put up money to buy Meredith's share of the business. Franklin was now the sole proprietor of his own print shop, and he aimed to make it the most successful in the colonies.

Print shops in colonial America often published their own newspapers, and Franklin was anxious to use his talents as a writer to launch a publication. The problem, however, was that there were already two newspapers in Philadelphia; Franklin knew a third would never survive. The competitors were Andrew Bradford's dull but profitable *American Weekly Mercury* and a slapdash, unreadable sheet with the self-important title of *The Universal Instructor in All Arts and Sciences and Pennsylvania Gazette*, which was published by Franklin's old boss, Samuel Keimer. Franklin could easily tell the *Universal Instructor* was the weaker of the two papers, so he concocted a scheme to put it out of business.

Using his talent as a writer, Franklin anonymously submitted a series of humorous essays to the *Mercury*, not unlike the Silence Dogood essays he had published in his brother's newspaper in Boston. Writing under the names Martha Careful and Celia Shortface, Franklin lampooned Keimer's newspaper, which at the time was filling its pages by reprinting an encyclopedia. Next, Franklin provided a number of anonymous essays in which he promised the *Mercury* readers a generous dose of Philadelphia gossip. Writing under the name "Busy-Body," Franklin actually offered little in the way of gossip, but he did take the opportunity to make a number of observations on current issues. He wrote the type of opinion pieces that are common in newspapers today, but the *Mercury* had never published anything like them. For example, Busy-Body endorsed the printing of paper currency, a radical notion at the time because most business was transacted with solid pieces of gold and silver. Franklin felt that if more money circulated in the colony, more businesses would prosper. He had Busy-Body make that point: "Those who are lovers of trade and delight to see manufacturers encouraged will be for having a large addition to our currency."[28]

As Franklin expected, the Busy-Body essays became the talk of Philadelphia and, as he also expected, the *Universal Instructor* was soon on the verge of going out of business. At that point, Franklin stepped in and bought the newspaper at a very cheap price. He shortened the title to *Pennsylvania Gazette* and began the process of remaking it into the most popular newspaper in the colonies.

FRANKLIN AND "DEAR DEBBY"

While making plans for his newspaper and printing business, Franklin took a brief break to start a family. Franklin's romance with Deborah Read had been interrupted by his two-year stay in London. When he returned to Philadelphia, he found that Deborah had married. In the meantime, Franklin met other women and fathered a son, William, out of wedlock.

As for Read, her marriage to pottery maker John Rogers ended quite abruptly, with Rogers running off to an island in the Caribbean. Meanwhile, Deborah's father, John Read, died and left his family with little money. The renewal of the romance between Benjamin Franklin and Deborah Read Rogers proved convenient for both parties. Deborah Read needed a prosperous husband; Franklin needed a mother for his infant son. In September 1730, they entered marriage under what is known as "common law" (see "The Franklins' Common-law Marriage" on page 48).

In addition to raising Franklin's son William, the couple had a son, Francis (who died of smallpox at

As a young journeyman printer in Philadelphia, Pennsylvania, Benjamin Franklin stayed at the home of John Read. It was there that he met Read's daughter, Deborah, shown in this rare portrait. The romance that developed between Franklin and Deborah Read would eventually lead to marriage.

the age of four), and a daughter, Sarah, whom the Franklins called "Sally." Over the years, Read proved to be a help around the business. She worked behind the counter of the print shop and kept the books, meaning she looked after debts owed to the shop. At home, she kept house, cooked meals, and stitched

The Franklins' Common-law Marriage

Benjamin and Deborah Franklin were never married before a clergyman or an official of the Pennsylvania colonial government empowered to unite couples. They simply started living together. Yet their union in 1730 was legal, as it would be legal today in Pennsylvania as well as many other states. They were considered married under what is known as "common law."

Common law is a concept that originated in England in medieval times. Laws that are "common" are made through custom and use, but may not necessarily be written down in a constitution or similar code. Common-law marriage became a custom in medieval England because clergymen and officials of the royal government found it difficult to travel great distances into remote corners of the kingdom to perform weddings, so residents of rural villages were permitted to marry without a ceremony under common law.

The Franklins resorted to a common-law union because of questions surrounding Deborah Franklin's first marriage in 1725 to pottery maker John Rogers. Just four months after the wedding, Rogers abandoned his wife. He

clothes. Franklin called her "dear Debby" and she called him "Pappy." Franklin later referred to her as "a good and faithful helpmate."[29]

is believed to have gone to a Caribbean island, where he is presumed to have died in a brawl. His fate, however, was never certain. With no proof of his death, Deborah could not legally marry another man. If she married again and Rogers returned, Deborah could be charged with bigamy, the crime of marrying more than one spouse at the same time. In colonial Pennsylvania, the penalty for bigamy was quite harsh—39 lashes with a whip and life imprisonment.

The Franklins solved Deborah's dilemma by marrying under common law. That way, if Rogers returned, there would be no legal proof of their union. Today, common-law marriages are still recognized as legal in 14 states: Alabama, Colorado, Georgia, Idaho, Iowa, Kansas, Montana, New Hampshire, Ohio, Oklahoma, Rhode Island, South Carolina, Texas, and Utah. Washington, D.C., also recognizes common-law marriages.

As for Rogers, he never did return and the Franklins remained married under common law until Deborah Franklin's death in 1774.

MAKING JOURNALISM HISTORY

Franklin filled his newspaper with all manner of humorous essays, commenting on public issues as well as the common habit of many people to make fools of themselves. Meanwhile, Franklin discovered what all good editors eventually discover: Stories about crime and scandal sell newspapers. The *Gazette* published stories about unfaithful wives and husbands seeking revenge, and Franklin peppered the *Gazette's* pages with stories about crimes against Philadelphia citizens and the trials of accused criminals. He found it hard to resist commenting on these cases. When a couple accused of child abuse was let off lightly by the judge, who ordered them burned on the hands as punishment, Franklin called the ruling "pathetic," adding that the accused parents "had not only acted contrary to the particular law of all nations, but had even broken the universal law of nature."[30]

The *Gazette* soon outsold the *Mercury* and became the most sought-after newspaper in the colonies. The *Gazette* was lively and fun to read. It was also scrappy. Franklin made it clear that the *Gazette* would be fair to all, but it would not shy away from a good fight. In 1731, he wrote, "If all printers were determined not to print anything till they were sure it would offend nobody, there would be very little printed."[31]

The *Gazette* was often a part of journalism history. In 1745, the newspaper was among the first publications in America to publish an illustration, using the woodcut technique to produce a drawing of Fort Louisbourg in Canada. Franklin published the illustration after a group of New Englanders defeated French troops, who had been using the fort to launch raids against the colonists' fishing boats. Since the landmark publication of the early woodcut images, pictures have become a routine part of newspaper journalism, although photography and other modern imaging techniques have long since replaced woodcuts.

The battle for Fort Louisbourg was one of many skirmishes that led to the French and Indian War, fought between 1754 and 1760. When the conflict arose, Franklin felt strongly that the British colonies would do well to band together and form a common defense against the French invaders and their Native American allies. He used his newspaper to support the common defense. On May 19, 1754, Franklin drew and published a crude illustration of a snake chopped into eight parts. Each part was labeled with the initials of the colonies: New England, Pennsylvania, New York, New Jersey, Maryland, Virginia, North Carolina, and South Carolina, along with the caption "Join or Die." The message was clear: For the colonies to survive the war, they had to join together in a common defense.

The drawing was the first political cartoon published in a newspaper. It paved the way for centuries of political commentary drawn and written by cartoonists, whose work is published every day on the editorial pages of America's newspapers.

POOR RICHARD

Franklin's print shop did more than just publish the *Gazette*. Books were still hard to come by in the colonies, so Franklin often found work producing titles for America's eager readers. In 1740, his shop published an edition of the novel *Pamela*, written by British author Samuel Richardson. *Pamela* tells the story of a young maid who marries her employer and wins acceptance in British society. It was the first work of fiction published by an American press.

Franklin also saw the value of expanding his business. As his older brother's ill-treated apprentice, Franklin certainly had an understanding of the struggles of the poorly-paid apprentice. Instead of mistreating his own apprentices, Franklin trained them in the printer's trade, sent them off to other cities, and provided them with money to establish their own shops. By the 1730s, former Franklin apprentices were running print shops in cities from Charleston, South Carolina, to Hartford, Connecticut. Of course, Franklin collected a share of their profits.

Perhaps Franklin's greatest achievement as a publisher, though, was his creation of *Poor Richard's Almanac,* an annual compilation of information on the calendar, astronomy, astrology, weather predictions, recipes, and assorted other useful facts. What set Franklin's almanac apart from the many others published in the colonial era was the humorous and homespun wisdom he wove throughout its pages during the 25 years the almanac remained in publication.

The first edition of the almanac appeared in 1732. Franklin named the almanac after the fictional Richard Saunders, a humble and common man who always had advice for humble and common men. "I consider'd it as a proper Vehicle for conveying Instruction among the common People, who bought scarce any other Books," Franklin wrote.[32] Over the years, Poor Richard

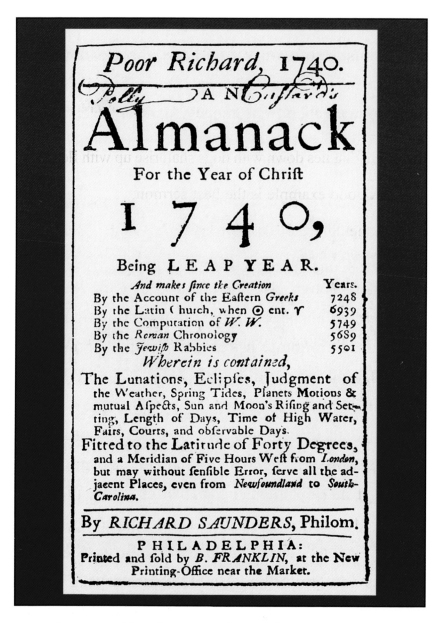

Featuring everything from weather and astronomy facts to tips on cooking and gardening, *Poor Richard's Almanac* quickly became one of Benjamin Franklin's most successful ventures. This is the title page for the 1740 edition.

dispensed many brief words of advice, the most famous of which is the often-quoted, "Early to bed and early to rise, makes a man healthy, wealthy and wise." Other well-known advice from Poor Richard included:

- He that lies down with dogs shall rise up with fleas.

- A good example is the best sermon.

- When the well's dry we know the worth of water.

- Haste makes waste.

- Love your enemies, for they will tell you your faults.

- Genius without education is like silver in the mine.

- Half the truth is often a great lie.

- God helps them that help themselves.[33]

The final edition *Poor Richard's Almanac* was published in 1757, written by Franklin as he sailed to England to represent Pennsylvania's interests before Parliament. The almanac became his most successful business venture, selling 10,000 copies a year. While there is no question that the writing in the almanac is witty, Franklin readily admitted that he borrowed most of Poor Richard's advice from other writers or from old-world proverbs, the authorship of which had long been forgotten. Typically, he would read a humorous phrase written by someone else and simply change a few words to make the expression his own. In the final edition of the almanac, Franklin admitted that "not a tenth part of the wisdom was my own."[34]

Test Your Knowledge

I What method did Franklin use to save money for books?

  a. He stole a few pennies from his brother James.

  b. He sold newspapers on the street.

  c. He limited himself to a vegetarian diet.

  d. All of the above.

2 Why did Franklin travel to England in 1724?

  a. To serve as a diplomat

  b. To buy a printing press

  c. To become a teacher

  d. To join the military

3 How did Franklin revolutionize American typography?

  a. He was the first American printer to manufacture type.

  b. He invented a new kind of press that used less ink.

  c. He was the first printer to print on both sides of a single page.

  d. None of the above.

4 How did Franklin gain control of the *Pennsylvania Gazette*?

    a. He borrowed money from Pennsylvania's governor.

    b. He accused the *Gazette* of treason against England.

    c. He wrote satirical letters to hurt the *Gazette*'s image and circulation.

    d. He bought the newspaper with funds from his brother James.

5 What was *Poor Richard's Almanac*?

    a. A series of satirical letters and columns authored by Franklin

    b. An annual publication featuring material on weather, astronomy, astrology, and recipes, as well as homespun wisdom

    c. A book lampooning the English monarchy

    d. None of the above

ANSWERS: 1. c; 2. b; 3. a; 4. c; 5. b

OUR RIGHTS AND OUR LIBERTIES

The Search for Useful Knowledge

By the 1740s, Benjamin Franklin's newspaper was the talk of the colonies, his *Poor Richard's Almanac* sold thousands of copies each year, and his other printing ventures helped make him wealthy and respected. For Franklin, it was time to "retire" from the printing business and turn matters over to trusted employees, although he certainly maintained ownership of his shop, contributed advice to his almanac readers, and occasionally penned an essay for the *Gazette*. Nevertheless, in 1748, Franklin said he was looking forward to a life of "leisure to read, study, [and] make experiments."[35] Franklin intended to devote himself to the pursuit of his true passion, the study of science and nature. A devoted tinkerer, he constantly made sketches and developed ideas for gadgets that would improve the quality of life while he also sought to understand the mysteries of nature.

Some of those mysteries would remain unsolved. For example, in 1754 Franklin observed a fly seemingly drown in a splash of Madeira wine, then come back to life after being exposed to sunlight. He wondered whether a man could also be submerged into a cask of wine for, say, 100 years, then brought back to life after exposure to sunlight. In fact, Franklin said he would be happy to give his theory a try, "having a very ardent desire to see and observe the state of America a hundred years hence."[36]

For the most part, though, Franklin's ideas and discoveries added a great deal to society's understanding of nature, and his inventions would become welcome additions to the colonial lifestyle.

Born in Boston and having made his home in Philadelphia, Franklin was well aware that winters in the Northeast could sometimes be brutally cold. In the colonial era, the only heat available in homes was through the fireplace. In actuality, though, fireplaces give off little heat because hot air rises and most of the heat escapes through the chimney. To keep truly warm, one must sit very close to the hearth.

Franklin wondered whether heat from the fire could be trapped and spread out in the room before it escaped through the chimney. In 1741, he designed what he called the "Pennsylvania fireplace," which has come to be known as the "Franklin stove." Built into the center of the room, the iron stove gave off heat in all directions. The air entered through vents while the smoke escaped through pipes built into the bottom, which then ran under the floor and up through the chimney.

The stove had its drawbacks. Because the fire burned in an enclosed space, it burned hotter, which means the wood was consumed quicker. The homeowner had to constantly toss wood into the stove or the fire would go out. The stove was still a vast improvement over an ordinary fireplace, and Franklin stove owners were delighted with them. One enthusiastic owner was the governor of Pennsylvania, who offered Franklin a patent on the stove, meaning that for many years the government would guarantee that Franklin collected a share of all profits made from the sale of Franklin stoves. Franklin turned down the patent and would, in fact, refuse patents for all of his inventions. Later, Franklin wrote, "As we enjoy great advantages from the invention of others, we should be glad of an opportunity to serve others by any invention of ours, and this we should do freely and generously."[37]

FRANKLIN THE "ELECTRICIAN"

Franklin was most fascinated by the properties of electricity—indeed, as an "electrician," he performed his most significant research. Electricians today are tradesmen who wire new homes and businesses, and ensure that electrical power is delivered safely to tools, computers, televisions, washing machines, water heaters, and other household appliances. In the colonial era, electricity had yet not been harnessed as a source of power and little was understood about its properties.

Benjamin Franklin's love of scientific experimentation and study made him one of the greatest innovators in history. This portrait highlights Franklin's experiments with electricity, which yielded such inventions as the lightning rod and the battery.

Electricians were scientists who conducted the initial experiments on electricity.

Scientists had known for years that they could generate a spark of static electricity by creating friction. Traveling entertainers often put on shows displaying various electrical tricks, such as dangling a boy from the ceiling by silk cords, then drawing sparks from the boy's fingers by rubbing his bare feet with glass tubes. In 1743, Franklin saw an entertainer put on such a show in Boston and immediately found himself dazzled by the display. Later, he bought the entertainer's equipment and set up an electrical laboratory in his home in Philadelphia. "I never before was engaged in any study that so totally engrossed my attention," he said.[38]

One of his devices was a spinning glass tube that produced an electrical spark. Franklin found that he could make the tube pass an electrical charge to a person, who could then pass the charge on to a second person. Franklin concluded that the friction of the spinning tube was not necessary for electricity to travel. Once the electricity was generated, it could travel from object to object, or person to person, as long as there was a means to "conduct" the charge.

At the time, Dutch inventor Pieter van Muschenbroek had developed a simple method of capturing an electrical charge and storing it in a glass jar. Van Muschenbroek named the device the "Leyden jar," after the town where he lived. The jar was wrapped in metal foil; inside was a small amount of water and a wire hook. The jar could hold a considerable charge. An electrician in France demonstrated the power of a Leyden jar by having 180 of King Louis XV's guards link hands, then making them all jump at once by delivering a spark from the jar to the first man in line.

The problem, however, was that nobody understood how the jar worked or how it could be used, other than to provide shocks for the entertainment of an audience. Franklin obtained a Leyden jar in 1747 and soon solved its riddles.

He determined that electrical currents contain equally "positive" and "negative" poles, and that positively charged currents can only continue to flow if they are linked to a negative receptor. He revised the design of the Leyden jars, linked them together by metal wire, positive pole to negative pole, and invented the world's first battery. Today, portable CD players, cell phones, flashlights, and thousands of other modern electrical devices receive their power under the principles developed by Franklin.

Of course, Franklin now had a battery, but he could not find a good use for it. Indeed, it would take another century before the first practical uses for electricity would be employed. The first transmission of telegraph messages occurred in 1844. The telephone arrived in 1876, the light bulb in 1879, and radio in 1895. As Franklin pursued his study of electricity, all those advancements were very much in the future. Soon after developing the battery, Franklin wrote to a friend that, while he continued to find the study of electricity fascinating, "we have hitherto been able to discover nothing in the way of use to mankind."[39] That would soon change.

KITE AND KEY

Franklin was not the first electrician to notice the curious similarities between the sparks of static electricity and the bolts of lightning that streaked across the sky during a thunderstorm. Franklin drew up a list of similarities, finding sparks and lightning to be the same in their color, swiftness, and sound—a "crack" made

The Leyden jars shown in this picture were used to store electrical energy. The modern battery owes its origins to the Leyden jar. These particular jars were acquired by Benjamin Franklin, who was always eager to collect instruments and devices that interested him.

when the current was exposed to air. He also believed that sparks and lightning were both attracted to metal, which he knew to be a good conductor. In November

1749, Franklin wrote that he intended to prove lightning was nothing more than a tremendous jolt of electricity. "Let the experiment be made," he wrote.[40]

Franklin believed the water vapor in the air during a thunderstorm acted as a conductor for the lightning, making it streak through the sky. He concluded that water vapor would gather around tall trees, masts of ships, and church steeples, and would draw the lightning more than objects on a flat surface. He advised people not to stand under trees during a thunderstorm—advice that remains sound today.

Franklin suggested that lightning could be tricked into striking a target that would not be affected by the jolt, thus saving the church steeple from destruction. He proposed an experiment: A long metal rod would be carried to the top of a tower and raised skyward during an electrical storm. When the water vapor gathered around the tower and attracted the lightning, the bolt would strike the metal rod, not the tower.

His idea for "drawing Lightning from the Clouds"[41] led to his invention of the lightning rod, a device that helped prevent countless fires in the crowded cities of Europe as well as in the colonies. To fashion a lightning rod, Franklin suggested a short iron pole be attached to the roof of the building, and that the rod be connected to the ground by means of a wire. Then, when lightning struck the rod, it would follow the wire into the ground, where the charge would be dispelled harmlessly. As with the Franklin stove, he turned down a patent for the lightning rod.

In June 1752, while the French were experimenting with his ideas, Franklin tried a similar experiment. Accompanied by his son William, Franklin lofted a kite made of silk into the dark skies of an electrical storm. Tied high to the kite was a metal wire; at the end of the kite string, Franklin fastened a heavy metal key. As it started to rain, Franklin took shelter in a nearby shed while William, then 21, ran across a field to loft the kite. Once William had the kite up in the air, he handed the string to his father. Franklin did not intend for the kite to take a direct jolt of lightning— he knew that would be dangerous—but believed the kite would pick up stray current from passing clouds. He was proven correct. As a cloud passed overhead, Franklin touched the key and felt a mild shock. The result of the experiment was published that October in the *Gazette,* and in the following year's *Poor Richard's Almanac,* Franklin gave instructions on

Benjamin Franklin is seen here with a kite and a key, in what may be the most recognized image of the inventor and statesman. This Currier & Ives print recounts the fateful day in 1752 when Franklin established that lightning could be attracted to certain objects during a storm.

how readers could conduct a kite and key experiment on their own.

Franklin did find a practical use for his experiments with electricity. By developing the lightning rod and the battery, Franklin took the first small steps toward harnessing and directing electrical power.

BIFOCALS AND STREET LAMPS

Electricity is only one area of science in which Franklin's contributions would have a lasting impact. In his later years, Franklin suffered from many ailments, including failing eyesight. In 1785, after years of wearing two pairs of spectacles—one to help him read, the other to help him see distant objects—he came up with the idea of combining the lenses from both pairs into a single pair of glasses, so that he would not have to constantly change glasses. Combining the two lenses turned out to be quite easy; he simply took the two pairs to a lens grinder, had each of the four lenses sliced in half, then had the bottom half of the reading lenses fit into the same frame as the top half of his distance lenses. He wrote, "I wear my spectacles constantly, I have only to move my eyes up or down, as I want to see distinctly far or near, the proper glasses being always ready."[42] He called the invention "Double Spectacles." The millions of people who use them today know them as "bifocals."

In 1941, a score for a string quartet of three violins and a cello surfaced in Paris. The composer, whose name was printed on the score, was "Benjamin Francklin." Historians have long debated whether this was the work of Franklin, whose name was misspelled for reasons unknown, or of someone else. There is no question, though, that Franklin harbored an appreciation for music—he played the guitar and harp—and in 1762 invented a musical instrument known as the "glass armonica" or "glassychord."

Franklin developed the idea after watching an entertainer play music on glasses that had been partially filled with water. The entertainer made the glasses vibrate by rubbing them with his fingers, and was able to coax different notes out of each glass. Franklin applied the principle to his glass armonica. He had a glassblower fashion 37 bowls of different sizes. Next, he rigged up a wheel operated by a foot pedal to spin the bowls on their sides—essentially, the same type of apparatus that turns a spool of yarn on a spinning wheel. He wet his fingers and applied them to the bowls as they spun, creating notes of music. The composers Mozart and Beethoven were so impressed with the sounds they heard from the armonica that they each composed music for the instrument. Twenty years after its invention, the armonica still dazzled music critics. In 1782, the *German Almanac of Music* declared, "Of all the musical inventions, the one of

Mr. Franklin of Philadelphia has created perhaps the greatest excitement."[43]

Franklin served as colonial postmaster, a job that required him to coordinate the activities of many coaches that carried mail. His couriers had to cover dozens of miles each day. To organize the routes, Franklin had roads marked with stones placed every mile. Cut into each stone was the distance from one destination to the next. To calculate a mile, he used an "odometer" that counted each time a wagon wheel made a complete spin. If the wheel was laid out in a linear distance, it would cover 13.2 feet, so the odometer counted each time the wagon traveled 13.2 feet. When the odometer counted exactly 400 spins of the wheel, the wagon had covered one mile. Although odometers had been employed as early as the year 15 B.C. by the Romans, Franklin's use of the device brought fresh innovation to the problem of accurately measuring distance.

During Franklin's lifetime, the streets in Philadelphia were lit at night by oil lamps. The flames burned in glass globes that stood atop iron posts. Franklin noticed that the soot from the burning oil fogged the globes, causing them to give off little light. He designed an oil lamp with slits in the bottom and a funnel-shaped pipe on top so that air would move upward through the lamp, allowing the smoke to escape. What's more, each side of the lamp was composed of a removable pane of glass; that way, if the glass fogged, a lamplighter could remove the panes for cleaning.

STUDIES OF WEATHER, VOLCANOES, AND INSECTS

Franklin was fascinated by natural science and made many observations of nature that would help explain changes in the weather, currents of the ocean, and even how insects communicate. For example, during his lifetime, he crossed the Atlantic Ocean eight times. Whenever he traveled, he took along a thermometer that he lowered over the side of the ship to determine the temperature of the water. His observations led him to conclude that the Gulf Stream was warmer than the rest of the Atlantic. The Gulf Stream is the current of water that originates in the tropical Gulf of Mexico and runs near the coastline of America north to the cold Canadian waters. What's more, Franklin found that by taking regular tests of water temperature, he could compose a chart of the ocean showing the path of the

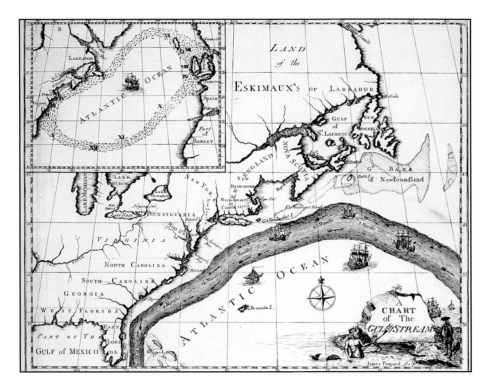

Among his many interests, Benjamin Franklin was fascinated by weather. This map shows his representation of the Gulf Stream, a strong Atlantic current that funnels warm water from south to north along America's eastern coastline. Ship captains used Franklin's map to find favorable currents and to avoid storms.

Gulf Stream. Because ships heading west were slowed when they ran into the quick, east-flowing current of the Gulf Stream, Franklin's chart was used by sea captains to plot courses that avoided tropical waters.

His study of weather led him to conclude that the big storms that hit the East Coast, known as "northeasters" because of their northeast-blowing winds, actually originate in the south. On October 21, 1743, Franklin intended to observe a lunar eclipse—an event in the

Daylight Savings Time

The custom of making better use of daylight hours by rising an hour earlier in spring and summer is known as Daylight Savings Time. The practice was first employed in 1916 in Germany and Austria during World War I. The United States tried Daylight Savings Time for a year in 1918, repealed it after the war, then readopted it in 1942 to save energy during World War II. Daylight Savings Time was again repealed in 1945. Since 1966, however, nearly all states have observed the shift in time. Residents are asked to set their clocks ahead by an hour in spring, then return to standard time in the fall.

Benjamin Franklin's ideas about making better use of daylight hours led to the concept of Daylight Savings Time. While living in France during the American Revolution, Franklin enjoyed staying up late to play chess with friends. One evening, Franklin and a friend had to take a pause from their game when the candles burned out. Franklin sent his friend to find more candles, but the fellow returned a few minutes later to report that candles

night sky when the Earth's shadow covers the moon, turning it orange. He was disappointed by the arrival of a storm that blackened the skies, covering up the event.

were unnecessary because daybreak had already arrived. The incident led Franklin to conclude that if people would rise earlier in the morning, they would save money on candles. He published an essay in France suggesting the idea, calling it his "Economical Project." He suggested that Parisians might save an "immense sum" by "the economy of using sunshine instead of candles."

Daylight Savings Time commences at 2 A.M. on the first Sunday in April and ends at 2 A.M. on the last Sunday in October. People are advised to adjust their clocks before going to bed on the Saturday night before the time shifts occur. Daylight Savings Time is not a national requirement: Hawaii and parts of Arizona and Indiana do not observe Daylight Savings Time.

In 2005, Congress proposed commencing Daylight Savings Time a month earlier and ending it a month later to save even more energy. In making the proposal, U.S. Representative Edward Markey of Massachusetts told a reporter for the *Wall Street Journal*, "The more daylight we have, the less electricity we use."

Franklin later read that the eclipse had been visible in Boston. He found this curious, because the storm that evening had been a northeaster. Shouldn't the storm have blacked out the eclipse in a city northeast of Philadelphia? Meanwhile, Franklin also read the storm caused damage to cities south of Philadelphia. By studying the weather conditions for the day in question, Franklin concluded that hot air blown north by winds from the south attracted cooler northeastern winds, creating the conditions for the northeaster. Modern meteorologists predict the weather by looking for the same signs in the atmosphere that Franklin found on the night his view of the lunar eclipse was spoiled.

In 1783, another study of the weather led Franklin to conclude that the ash spit out during volcanic erup-tions—he called it "summer fog"—could often cloud the atmosphere for months, blocking out sunshine and causing some areas of the planet to experience cold winters. He blamed a volcano in Iceland for causing that year's very harsh winter in Europe.

According to one story, in 1748, Franklin found ants had gotten into a pot of molasses that had been sit-ting on the floor. He shook the ants out of the pot, then hung the pot from the ceiling by a string but purposely left one ant remaining in the pot. Soon, after the ant had eaten its fill, the little fellow found his way out of the pot, up the string, across the ceiling, and down the wall. Later, Franklin saw a parade of ants make their way to the molasses following the path the original ant had taken home. Obviously, Franklin concluded, ants could communicate—the first ant told his mates how to find the molasses.

By 1759, Franklin's accomplishments in the arts and sciences had become so well-known that he was awarded an honorary doctorate of laws by the University of St. Andrews, located on the remote North Sea coast of Scotland. Founded in the early fifteenth century, St. Andrews still exists today as an institute of higher learning. It is the oldest university in Scotland and the third-oldest in the English-speaking world. Franklin—who had only two years of formal schooling—was quite taken with St. Andrews' offer of the degree, and after he received the doctorate, he went by the name of "Doctor" Franklin. The citation on the degree read:

Whereas the ingenious and worthy Benjamin Franklin has . . . by his ingenious inventions and successful experiments enriched science . . . and more especially . . . electricity which heretofore was little known . . . we grant him all the privileges and honors which are anywhere granted to Doctors of Laws.[44]

Test Your Knowledge

I Which of the following inventions is attributed to Benjamin Franklin?
   a. The lightning rod
   b. The battery
   c. The "glassychord"
   d. All of the above

2 How did Franklin improve on the design of the Leyden jar?
   a. He determined that electrical currents contain positive and negative poles.
   b. He linked several Leyden jars together.
   c. Both a and b.
   d. None of the above.

3 Why did Franklin believe lightning was attracted to church steeples?
   a. He felt it was a sign from God.
   b. He thought that water vapor in the air, especially around tall objects, conducted lightning.
   c. He believed that the ringing of the church bells called the electricity down from the clouds.
   d. None of the above.

4 How much did Franklin earn through patents on his inventions?

   a. Franklin refused to accept patents and shared his inventions freely

   b. 1,000 gold coins

   c. 10,000 English pounds

   d. An acre of land for each practical invention

5 To which of the following sciences did Franklin contribute?

   a. Entomology (the study of insects)

   b. Meteorology (the study of weather)

   c. Volcanology (the study of volcanoes)

   d. All of the above

ANSWERS: 1. d; 2. c; 3. b; 4. a; 5. d

OUR RIGHTS AND OUR LIBERTIES

Community Organizer

In 1743, this advertisement appeared on the pages of the *Gazette*: "Lost at the late fire on Water Street, two leather buckets, marked B. Franklin & Co. Whoever brings them to the printer hereof shall be satisfied for their trouble."[45] The buckets were, in fact, owned by Benjamin Franklin, who had misplaced them while helping to douse a blaze as a member of the Union Fire Company, the first fire company in Philadelphia.

Franklin was the main force behind the formation of the fire company and remained a devoted member until the end of his life. Except for the years he spent out of the country as a diplomat, Franklin rarely missed a meeting of the fire company and was always sure to tote his two leather buckets to the meetings, which was the habit of all members.

Franklin got the idea for the fire company in 1736 while on a visit to Boston, where he witnessed a group of men—an organized "firefighting club"— working together to douse a blaze. In Philadelphia, fighting fires had been a haphazard undertaking. The people who pitched in to douse a burning building usually consisted of anyone who was nearby when the blazes erupted.

Franklin observed an "order and method"[46] around the scene of the fire in Boston. When he returned to Philadelphia, he aimed to organize the city's first fire company. He wrote a charter for the company, established a set of rules, and declared that the membership would meet once a month "for a social evening together discussing and communicating such ideas as occurred to us on the subject of fires."[47]

Interest in the Union Fire Company quickly spread throughout Philadelphia. Members signed up; funds were raised to purchase buckets, ladders, and pumps; and the company practiced regularly. Even as the founder of the company, Franklin worked as hard as everyone else, manning the hand pumps and passing buckets. What's more, he used the pages of his newspaper to encourage people to be conscious of fire hazards around their homes, often warning Philadelphians to keep their chimneys clean.

There were so many applicants for membership that volunteers had to be turned away. Franklin urged them to form their own fire companies, which did occur. In fact, the network of fire companies born with Franklin's Union Fire Company formed the beginnings of what would become a professional fire department under the management of the city government.

THE JUNTO

More than any other American of his era, Franklin realized that Americans were members of their own community, separate from England and the other

European countries of their ancestors. To thrive in the New World, Franklin believed Americans needed to work together as a community. Franklin organized and supported a number of local and national institutions, all conceived to make colonists' lives better and safer.

The first organization Franklin helped form was the "Leather Apron Club," otherwise known as the "Junto." The name was drawn from the Spanish word *junta*, which means "meeting." Established in 1727 with the participation of a number of young Philadelphia tradesmen, Franklin intended the organization to be a service club—its aim was to undertake projects for the betterment of the community—but it was mostly a social club where members debated public issues.

One of the first ideas hatched by the Junto was the establishment of a library. Even though Franklin was now a man of means and could well afford to buy books, new volumes were still scarce in Philadelphia and other cities. To share their books, members of the Junto pooled their volumes and created a small library. In 1731, Franklin took the idea of a library a step further and proposed the formation of the Library Company of Philadelphia. The Library Company would be supported by paid subscriptions. Members were expected to pay a small annual sum for the right to borrow books.

Over time, as the collection grew, Franklin noticed that membership in the Library Company helped turn his fellow Junto members and other residents of the city into devoted readers. Soon, cities in other colonies started their own subscription libraries. "These libraries have improved the general conversation of the Americans, and made the common tradesmen and farmers as intelligent as most gentlemen from other countries," he wrote.[48] In Philadelphia, the Library Company has continued to grow over the years and remains an important institution in the city. Today the library owns 500,000 volumes and 160,000 manu-scripts, including some of the original books that were bought in 1731.

REFORMING THE NIGHT WATCH
AND PAVING THE STREETS

In colonial times, the job of policing fell into the hands of constables appointed by local city officials. The constables were left with the job of organizing "night watches"—citizen patrols to keep the city streets safe at night. The system was largely corrupt, with constables giving the night jobs to friends who did more drinking than patrolling. Many constables accepted bribes from neighborhood men who didn't want to join the night watches. By 1752, Franklin had been elected to a seat in the Pennsylvania Assembly, the governing body of the colony. After talking over the problem with members of the Junto, Franklin proposed a solution to the night watch problem that was adopted by the legislative body: fees for the night watches would be raised through taxes. By taking over the responsibility of paying for the night watches, the Pennsylvania Assembly could guard against the corrupt practices of the local constables. Franklin wrote:

> The city watch was one of the first things that I conceived to want regulation. It was managed by the constables of the respective wards in turn; the constable warned a number of housekeepers [householders] to attend him for the night. Those who chose never to attend paid him six shillings a year to be excused, which was supposed to be for hiring substitutes, but was in reality much more than was necessary for that purpose, and made the

constableship a place for profit; and the constable, for a little drink, often got such ragamuffins about him as a watch that respectable housekeepers did not choose to mix with. Walking the rounds, too, was often neglected and most of the nights spent in tippling.[49]

Franklin joined the Pennsylvania Assembly in 1751, winning a seat that opened due to the death of a long-time member. "I conceived my becoming a member would enlarge my powers of doing good," he said.[50] Following his reform of the night watch, he used his position on the assembly to draw up a plan for paving Philadelphia's streets—well into the eighteenth century, many of the city's streets were unpaved, and when it rained they became a muddy mess. A tax was adopted by the assembly, with the proceeds going toward paving Philadelphia's streets.

THE POST OFFICE

In 1753, Franklin received an appointment from Parliament to serve as deputy postmaster of the colonies. Franklin, along with another deputy post-master, William Hunter of Virginia, would be charged with running the postal service throughout the colonies. Franklin attacked the job with enthusiasm. He intended to streamline delivery of the mail, speeding up the time it took for letters to circulate throughout the colonies.

He started by making a 1,600-mile tour to inspect all post offices in the colonies and concluded that the mail could move faster. He ordered the couriers to ride day and night, using lanterns in darkness to light their way. His use of the odometer led to the establishment

The Pennsylvania Militia

Pennsylvania was founded in 1681 by William Penn and other members of the Society of Friends, or Quakers, who sought to escape religious persecution in England. A basic belief held by the Quakers is their strict commitment to pacifism. Quakers oppose all wars and often, on religious grounds, refuse to bear arms.

By 1747, Pennsylvania—like all the colonies—found itself facing an increasing threat from the French and Indians, but the Pennsylvania Assembly, which was dominated by Quakers, refused to establish a militia to protect the colony from the invaders. Benjamin Franklin bristled at the Assembly's refusal to protect the colony's residents and, using the *Gazette* to publicize his idea, proposed that of new and shorter routes between cities. Franklin's innovations soon made a difference. In time, the post office under Franklin was able to take a letter written in Philadelphia, deliver it to New York, and then deliver the reader's response back to Philadelphia—all within 24 hours.

Franklin also established the "dead letter" office—a place where undeliverable mail is sent to be opened. At the dead letter office, the correspondence is destroyed

Pennsylvanians form their own militia, independent of the colonial government.

Franklin soon announced plans for public meetings to sign up members and was shocked when his call to arms resulted in 10,000 Pennsylvania men volunteering for duty. The volunteers contributed their own money, which paid for guns, cannons, and ammunition.

Because Franklin founded the militia, he was offered the rank of colonel, but he turned it down because he had no military experience and knew nothing about tactics or how to lead men into battle. Instead, he accepted the rank of a common soldier and fulfilled his obligation by walking guard duty along the Delaware River.

and any other contents, if they have value, are auctioned to the public. Today, some 57 million letters and packages a year end up in the U.S. Postal Service's "mail recovery centers," which are otherwise known as the dead letter offices.

Perhaps his greatest contribution to the postal service was helping bring Americans closer together. By speeding up the methods of communication among residents of the colonies, Franklin helped set the stage for the sense of community that would become so important in the future, as notions of independence started flowing among the colonies.

A UNIVERSITY FOR PENNSYLVANIA

One idea that Franklin raised among his fellow Junto members was a way to improve the education of young people in Pennsylvania. In 1749, Franklin laid out his ideas on education in a pamphlet titled *Proposals Relating to the Education of Youth in America*. In the pamphlet, he pointed out that there was no college in Pennsylvania and that the colleges in other colonies—Harvard in Massachusetts, Princeton in New Jersey, Yale in Connecticut, and William and Mary in Virginia—were predominantly church-based institutions

Benjamin Franklin was well aware of the importance of education. He envisioned an institution that would emphasize a secular education in mathematics, science, literature, business, and athletics. Franklin's "Philadelphia Academy" (shown here) opened in 1751, and later became known as the University of Pennsylvania.

in which worship and religious studies were emphasized. Franklin envisioned a school that would teach much more practical skills in mathematics, history, business, and speech-making and debate. He also hoped athletics would be a part of education, that students would exercise by "running, leaping, wrestling and swimming."[51] He hoped that some of the academy's graduates would take up teaching as a career, so that they would be "qualified to act as Schoolmasters in the Country, to teach Children Reading, Writing, Arithmetick, and the Grammar of their Mother Tongue."[52]

In 1750, Franklin drew up a charter for the school and convinced some friends and business leaders to contribute money to the institution. In 1751, with Franklin serving as president of the board, "Philadelphia Academy" opened its doors to its first students. In 1791, the name of the school was changed to the University of Pennsylvania. Today it is regarded as one of the most prestigious colleges in America.

COMMUNITY OF AMERICANS

Franklin's interests were varied—they ranged from protecting communities by organizing fire companies and night watches to the founding of a college that would educate young people.

At some point during the 1700s, Franklin and other colonists started thinking of themselves not only as subjects of the British crown, but also as "Americans." One of the places where this idea was first discussed was in the meetings of the American Philosophical

Society. Franklin intended this group to be an expansion of the Junto. That group was composed of Philadelphia tradesmen and other city residents, and mostly confined itself to matters of local importance, such as the fire company and university. Franklin thought a similar group composed of leaders from all of the colonies could work together on ideas that would have a more widespread impact. He wanted it to cover all aspects of colonial life—from farming and trade to science and the arts.

Writing in 1743, Franklin stated,

The first drudgery of settling new colonies is now pretty well over, and there are many in every province in circumstances that set them at ease, and afford leisure to cultivate the finer arts, and improve the common stock of knowledge.[53]

A year later, the American Philosophical Society held its first meeting. The founding members of the society included doctors, lawyers, clergymen, merchants, and scientists. The meetings were irregular, and Franklin often complained that members seemed to have just minimal interest in the society. They are

Home of the American Philosophical Society since the 1780s, this sturdy building continues to serve the purpose for which it was built more than 200 years ago. It is located at Fifth and Chestnut streets in Philadelphia, Pennsylvania.

"very idle Gentlemen; they take no Pains,"[54] he once said. But when the members did find time to meet, they offered ideas on improving farming and medicine, and took interest in scientific pursuits, such as physics, astronomy, and mathematics.

Later, as the notion of breaking away from English rule started circulating in the colonies, members of the society suggested that America had the economic strength to prosper on its own and that it was no longer dependent on England for its survival. It was during this period that the membership of the organization grew to include such men as George Washington, John Adams, Thomas Jefferson, Alexander Hamilton, Thomas Paine, and James Madison—who, along with Franklin, would play important roles in the establishment of America not only as a community, but as a country apart from England.

THE ALBANY PLAN

During this era, the American colonists were still steadfastly independent. Even as the colonies faced threats from the French and their Native American allies during the French and Indian War (1754–1763), leaders of the individual colonies were wary of one another and hesitant to meddle in each other's affairs. As such, there was very little history of cooperation among the colonies. With the threat posed by the war, Franklin was among the first of the colonial leaders to realize that a common defense and cooperation in military strategy would benefit all of the colonies. That philosophy had prompted Franklin to sketch his "Join or Die" cartoon in the *Gazette*.

In 1754, Franklin was among the delegates selected to participate in the "Albany Congress," a meeting that the governor of New York and business leaders in England had set up in the city of Albany with leaders of the Iroquois tribe to hear the Indians' complaints. At the time, the war was not going well for the colonists—the French had just defeated an army under George Washington at a battle in Ohio. Writing in the *Gazette*, Franklin charged that Washington's military defeat was due to "the present disunited state of the British colonies."[55] At the Albany Congress in June, the delegates made promises to the Iroquois, telling them they would be included in trade and that no new settlements would be built on their land without first consulting them. The Indians accepted the guarantees made in Albany, but Franklin feared that they would continue to ally themselves with the French. He wrote, "We brightened the chain with them, but in my opinion no assistance is to be expected from them in any dispute with the French until by a complete union among ourselves we are able to support them in case they should be attacked."[56]

Franklin presented to the delegates what became known as the "Albany Plan"—a blueprint for the establishment of a common government among the colonies that would address common needs and concerns. The Albany Plan did not advocate revolution—that notion was still more than two decades in the future. The delegates approved the plan, but stipulated that all colonial governments as well as the English Parliament would have to adopt Franklin's blueprint. But all the colonial governments rejected the Albany Plan, and Parliament turned it down as well.

Despite this early rejection of a common government, Americans would soon find that English laws and demands were becoming more and more repressive, and they would have no choice but to form a common defense.

Test Your Knowledge

1   How did Benjamin Franklin revolutionize fire fighting in Philadelphia?

     a. He invented a new type of leather bucket.

     b. He created and organized the first volunteer fire company.

     c. He developed a system of canals in the streets to provide water.

     d. None of the above.

2   What was the "Junto"?

     a. A group of local tradesmen seeking to improve their community through innovations and reforms

     b. A group of political revolutionaries seeking independence for the colonies

     c. A secret religious society

     d. None of the above

3   Which of the following innovations did Franklin introduce to postal delivery?

     a. Travel of postal workers by night, using lanterns

     b. Creation of a "dead letter" office for lost mail

     c. Use of the odometer to calculate shorter, faster routes between cities

     d. All of the above

4 How did the Philadelphia Academy (now the University of Pennsylvania) differ from its counterparts such as Harvard and Yale?

a. The academy emphasized secular pursuits such as mathematics and business over religious education.

b. The academy openly opposed British rule of the colonies.

c. The academy was the first educational institution to be financially profitable.

d. None of the above.

5 What was the "Albany Plan"?

a. A system of canals

b. A treaty with the Iroquois

c. An early proposal to unite the colonies under a common government

d. A design for a network of paved roads

ANSWERS: 1. b; 2. a; 3. d; 4. a; 5. c

Diplomat
and Patriot

Thomas Jefferson finished the first draft of the Declaration of Independence on June 21, 1776. Jefferson served as a delegate to the Continental Congress from Virginia. He had been appointed to head the committee charged with writing the document stating the colonists' reasons for declaring independence from the English king.

Jefferson spent several days writing in the second-floor room of an inn on Market Street in Philadelphia, just blocks from Benjamin Franklin's house. Franklin, a delegate to the Congress from Pennsylvania, was also on Jefferson's committee, but during the summer of 1776, Franklin was forced to spend a lot of time in bed. Then 70 years old, Franklin suffered from gout, a painful disease of the joints that often affects the ability to walk.

Franklin was in no shape to take a direct hand in drafting the declaration, but Jefferson, who was then just 33 years old, respected Franklin's wisdom and wanted his input on the document. When Jefferson finished the draft, he sent it to Franklin's home with this note: "Will Doctor Franklin be so kind as to peruse it and suggest such alterations as his more enlarged view of the subject will dictate?"[57]

Franklin had spent a lifetime as a printer, writer, and editor and was, therefore, highly qualified to judge the declaration's power to communicate ideas. He read Jefferson's work and made just a few changes. For example, in his first draft of the declaration, Jefferson wrote, "We hold these truths to be sacred and undeniable, that all men are created equal . . ." Franklin

This image, depicting the drafting of the Declaration of
Independence, shows Benjamin Franklin (standing at left)
with Thomas Jefferson, John Adams, Roger Sherman, and
Robert R. Livingstone. Franklin's role as statesman was
integral to the organization and growth of the United States.

changed the sentence to read, "We hold these truths to be self-evident . . ."

Franklin changed just a few words but the difference was significant. By using the word *sacred*, Jefferson implied that equality was based on religious principles—probably not the best choice of words for a nation whose founders would stress separation of church and state. By changing the sentence to read "self-evident," Franklin clearly suggested that equality was the natural right of every individual.

Franklin's changes were included in the draft sent to the Continental Congress on July 2. The final vote occurred on July 4, and later that summer, the delegates signed the document. John Hancock, the delegate from Massachusetts who served as president of the Congress, signed with a broad signature that has become one of the most familiar symbols in American history. Nineteenth-century historian Jared Sparks wrote that when Hancock signed he urged all the delegates to remain committed to independence. "There must be no pulling different ways," Hancock was said to have warned. "We must all hang together."[58] According to Sparks, when Franklin realized the delegates had gambled their lives on the cause, he replied,

"Yes, we must, indeed, all hang together, or most assuredly, we shall all hang separately."[59]

PUBLIC SERVICE

Printer; journalist; scientist; founder of a fire company, a philosophical society, and a great university—had these been his only accomplishments, Franklin would be regarded as one of colonial America's greatest visionaries. In fact, Franklin was destined to make even greater contributions to the founding of the United States and the establishment of its laws. Franklin's career in public service spanned more than 40 years, starting in 1748 when he was elected to the Philadelphia city council and ending just before his death in 1790. He helped Thomas Jefferson, then the Secretary of State, resolve a border dispute with Canada shortly before he died. In the meantime, Franklin served as a member of the Pennsylvania Assembly, the Continental Congress, and the Constitutional Convention, and held a variety of other posts in public service.

There is no question that Franklin's contributions to the Declaration of Independence and the U.S. Constitution are important. In both cases, however, he acted more as a guiding hand and sounding board for the ideas of Jefferson and the other Founding Fathers than as an authoritative voice in shaping the nation's two most important documents. Franklin had never been shy about airing his opinions on any number of issues in his newspaper, but when it came to drafting a public document that would be debated and amended, Franklin preferred to work behind the scenes. "I have made it a rule," Franklin said, "whenever in my power, to avoid becoming the draftsmen of papers to be reviewed by a public body."[60]

Franklin attended the 1787 Constitutional convention in Philadelphia with ideas about how he wanted to see the government shaped, but few of his notions made it into the final body of laws. For example, Franklin favored a single legislative body rather than a "bicameral" system, which includes the House and the Senate. He opposed election of a president and instead favored an executive board. He opposed payment of salaries to elected officials and, when he lost that argument, also opposed granting officeholders the power to raise their own salaries. He lost that argument as well. Still, his presence at the convention as the nation's most elder statesmen helped calm nerves and smooth over trouble spots. When the convention reached an impasse on how the states were to be represented in Congress, Franklin helped forge the compromise that resulted in the election of two members from each state to the Senate and representation in the House based on population.

George Washington presided over the Constitutional Convention, taking his seat before the delegates in a chair that featured the carved image of a sun. At the conclusion of the convention, as the delegates lined up to sign the new nation's body of laws, Franklin made this observation: "I have often in the course of the session . . . looked at that behind the President without being able to tell whether it was rising or setting. But now at length I have the happiness to know that it's a rising and not a setting sun."[61]

AN AMERICAN ABROAD

Perhaps his greatest contributions to the founding of America, though, came from Franklin's serving as a diplomat abroad. From 1757 to 1762 and from 1764 to 1775, he represented the interests of Pennsylvania and other colonies in England; and from 1776 to 1785, Franklin served as American ambassador to France, the American colonies' closest ally in their struggle for independence.

Franklin made his first trip to England on Pennsylvania's behalf to argue for Parliament to impose taxes on lands owned by the heirs of William Penn. Throughout the first half of the eighteenth century, the Pennsylvania Assembly maintained a testy relationship with the "proprietors"—the heirs of the colony's founder who had been granted enormous areas of land. The assembly wanted the Penns to pay taxes on the land, but the property remained tax-free since William Penn had been granted the land by King Charles II in 1681 to repay a debt the king owed Penn's father. In 1756, royal governor William Denny vetoed a bill by the Pennsylvania Assembly to tax the Penn lands. The assembly decided it could no longer tolerate the situation. In January 1757, the assembly sent Franklin to England to argue its case before Parliament.

Deborah Franklin did not accompany her husband. Throughout his travels as postmaster or on other trips in the service of the Pennsylvania Assembly, Deborah always stayed home to look after her husband's many business interests. This time would be no different. Deborah hated to travel and was particularly frightened of sea travel. She stayed behind for what would turn out to be a five-year separation from her husband.

Arriving in London, Franklin found a home at 36 Craven Street, where he boarded with a widow, Margaret Stevenson, and her daughter, Polly, with whom he would develop a close friendship. He even using his correspondence with the girl to sketch out some of his ideas about electricity and other discoveries.

REPRESENTING THE COLONIES

Franklin settled the Penn taxation issue; in 1760, Parliament approved a bill that permitted the Pennsylvania Assembly to tax the Penn family's properties. Although the taxation issue was resolved, Franklin remained in London for another two years, becoming a well-respected figure around the English capital. He conducted experiments on electricity in the Craven Street house and set up a small press where he published a humorous newspaper he called the *Craven Street Gazette*. He took trips to the continent, where he met many of Europe's important statesmen and scientists, and he participated in a study of farming methods headed by an English scientific society. In 1761, he attended the coronation of King

George III. Finally, in 1762, Franklin reluctantly returned to Philadelphia.

His son, William, had accompanied him on the trip. While staying in London, William Franklin married an English-born woman, Elizabeth Downes. William, who had been educated as a lawyer, elected to remain in London with his new wife, but late in 1762 he was appointed royal governor of New Jersey. That year, William returned to America as the king's main representative in the colony of New Jersey.

Benjamin Franklin's return to Philadelphia would turn out to be quite brief, for the Pennsylvania Assembly valued his diplomatic skills and, in 1764, sent him back to England to represent the colony's interests before Parliament. Soon, Georgia, New Jersey, and Massachusetts appointed him to oversee their interests before Parliament as well. Again, Deborah stayed behind in Philadelphia. Franklin happily moved back in with Margaret and Polly Stevenson, although by now they had moved up the street a few doors to 7 Craven Street.

It was during his second tenure in England that Franklin grew more hostile toward the British government. He became convinced that the colonies would be better off independent of England. Still, he constantly tried to smooth over troubles between the American colonies and England.

Franklin and His Son, William

When war erupted between England and the American colonies, Benjamin Franklin's son, William, remained loyal to the king. William had accompanied his father to England in 1757, where he won an appointment by King George III as royal governor of New Jersey. He served in that post until he was arrested by New Jersey patriots in January 1776 and placed under house arrest.

William was soon taken to Connecticut, where he was held in prison for two years. Freed in 1779, William moved to New York, where he joined an association of loyalists. As an outcast and supporter of the losing side, William finally left America in 1782 and returned to England, where he lived out his life. He died in 1813.

Benjamin Franklin maintained a close relationship with his son and was deeply hurt by William's decision to remain loyal to England. In a 1784 letter to William, excerpted in author Willard Randall's 1984 book, *A Little Revenge: Benjamin Franklin and His Son*, Franklin wrote, "Nothing has ever hurt me so much and affected

The incident that prompted the Pennsylvania Assembly to send Franklin back to England was Parliament's adoption of the Stamp Act—the first

me with such keen sensibilities as to find myself deserted in my old age by my only son; and not only deserted, but to find him taking up arms against me in a cause wherein my good fame, fortune and life were all at stake."

Franklin punished William by leaving him out of his will. When he died, Franklin left most of his considerable fortune to his daughter, Sally. To William, Franklin left little more than some land in Canada that was essentially worthless because others had already claimed ownership of it. Franklin said he decided to deprive William of his inheritance because, had England won the war, Franklin probably would have been hanged and had all his of property stripped from his ownership. Therefore, Franklin said, if William had his way and England won, there would have been nothing to leave him anyway. As reported in Walter Isaacson's 2003 book, *Benjamin Franklin: An American Life*, Franklin stated, "The part he acted against me in the late war, which is of public notoriety, will account for my leaving him no more of an estate he endeavored to deprive me of."

general tax levied on the colonists by the English government. Parliament imposed the tax because of the expense of keeping troops in the colonies during the French and Indian War and, following the treaty with France that ended the war, protecting the colonists from the occasional attacks by hostile Indians. Indeed, some 6,000 English troops had been permanently stationed in the colonies since the end of the French and Indian War. Under the law passed by Parliament, all legal documents, contracts, newspapers, pamphlets, and even playing cards had to include a stamp purchased from a tax collector, with the money returning to England.

Franklin thought the tax was unfair, but counseled the colonies to accept the Stamp Act because he believed wealthy colonists would bear most of the burden of paying the tax, while it would have little impact on ordinary citizens. (The tax was steepest on contracts written to conduct business; the larger the contract, the higher the tax.) Said Franklin, "It will operate as a general tax on the colonies, and yet not an unpleasing one. The rich, who handle most money, would in reality pay most of the tax."[62] Still, after returning to England, Franklin urged Parliament to repeal the Stamp Act and his arguments played a role in the English government's decision to revoke the tax.

There is no question that relations between England and the colonies were quickly deteriorating. Over the next several years, Parliament imposed new taxes on the colonies, troops were quartered in colonists' homes, and other rights of the colonists were suppressed. In 1773, patriots in Boston protested an English tax by dumping 342 chests of tea into Boston Harbor—the so-called Boston Tea Party.

A year later, Franklin weathered a scandal in which he was accused of leaking to newspapers letters written by Thomas Hutchinson, royal governor of Massachusetts, who called for repression of unrest in the colony. Summoned before Parliament, Franklin was denounced as a thief and a man without honor, but he stood up to the criticism and published a paper titled *Rules by Which a Great Empire May be Reduced to a Small One*, in which he set forth many of the points that would be raised in the Declaration of Independence. As the pamphlet circulated in England, Franklin wrote home to his sister, "I have held up a Looking-Glass in which some of the Ministers may see their ugly faces, and the Nation its Injustice."[63] By the spring of

1775, his welcome worn out, Franklin left England, apparently just ahead of an order for his arrest.

FRANKLIN IN FRANCE

Just before leaving England, Franklin received terrible news in a letter from his son William. Franklin's wife Deborah, who had been ill for a number of years, died shortly before Christmas in 1774. She had suffered a stroke in 1770 and, over the next four years, slowly lost her strength. "I find myself growing very feeble very fast," she wrote in 1772.[64]

When Franklin arrived home in May 1775, he found a fervor for rebellion in the colonies. Just a month before, the first shots had been fired at Lexington and Concord in Massachusetts, marking the first skirmishes between British soldiers and American colonists. Franklin was immediately appointed by the Pennsylvania Assembly to the Continental Congress, which selected him postmaster general of the colonies. He was also appointed to committees to oversee foreign policy, supply provisions to the army, and draft the Declaration of Independence.

Soon after the Declaration was adopted and signed, Franklin was dispatched to France, where he served

Benjamin Franklin, seen here at left, served as America's first ambassador to France, a nation that proved to be a critical ally in America's struggle for independence from Great Britain.

as ambassador to the colonies' closest ally. As ambassador, Franklin convinced the Comte de Vergennes, the skeptical French foreign minister, to make huge loans to the colonies and otherwise support the revolution by supplying soldiers, officers, guns, ships, and many other resources to the American cause. Meanwhile, Franklin became an immensely popular figure in France. The French people found themselves smitten with his charm and impressed with his scientific accomplishments, and Franklin in turn mixed well in French society.

While living in France, Franklin occupied a grand estate loaned to him by wealthy merchant Jacques-Donatien Leray de Chaumont, who was an enthusiastic supporter of the American Revolution. De Chaumont's estate was in the village of Passy, just outside Paris. Franklin was accompanied to France by his grand-children—16-year-old William Temple Franklin, who served as Franklin's secretary, and 7-year-old Benjamin Franklin Bache, who went to a nearby boarding school. Franklin was very fond of the boy, and called him "Benny."

During his stay in France, Franklin grew passionate about ballooning. In fact, Franklin and Benny Bache were standing in the crowd along the Seine River when the era of manned flight was born. Jean Pilatre de Rozier and the Marquis Francois d'Arlandes made the first untethered balloon flight, soaring to an altitude of a few hundred feet and traveling, downwind, about five miles before coming to a gentle landing just outside Paris. "I was then in great pain for the men, thinking them in danger of being thrown out or burnt," Franklin wrote.[65]

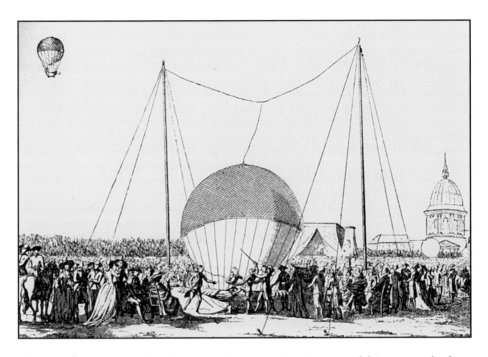

Always fascinated by innovation, Benjamin Franklin attended one of the first balloon ascents in 1783. When a skeptic asked Franklin what use this new technology could have, Franklin replied, "What is the use of a newborn baby?"

Franklin became an enthusiastic supporter of ballooning, believing it would "increase the power of man over matter."[66] As someone with a background in the postal service, he was delighted when he later received a letter delivered by a balloonist from England—the first letter delivered by air mail in history. As Franklin watched balloons float over Paris, he believed mankind was on the threshold of an important breakthrough that would revolutionize travel and bring people closer together.

Of course, even Franklin could not foresee the advances in aeronautics that were on the horizon. Those advances would culminate more than a century later in the first powered airplane flight of the Wright brothers, Orville and Wilbur, in Kill Devil Hills, North Carolina, in 1903. There is no question, however, that Franklin knew flight would not be confined to the sport of ballooning. In Paris, while witnessing a balloon float skyward, Franklin overheard a spectator who asked what use could there be for ballooning. Franklin turned to the man and responded, "What is the use of a new-born baby?"[67]

Test Your Knowledge

1 Why did Thomas Jefferson seek Franklin's advice on the wording of the Declaration of Independence?

   a. He believed Franklin was a better writer.

   b. He respected Franklin's wisdom and valued his input.

   c. The Declaration had originally been Franklin's idea.

   d. None of the above.

2 Which of the following provisions of the U.S. Constitution did Franklin oppose?

   a. A bicameral legislature consisting of two bodies (House and Senate)

   b. The office of president

   c. The ability of legislators to vote themselves pay increases

   d. All of the above

3 In which countries did Franklin serve as a diplomat?

   a. England and Spain

   b. Spain and France

   c. France and England

   d. None of the above

4   Why did Franklin encourage the colonies to accept the Stamp Act?

a. Because most of the tax would be paid by the wealthy

b. Because he feared war with England

c. Because he stood to profit directly from the tax

d. None of the above

5   As ambassador to France, Franklin persuaded the French to support the American colonies against the British by providing which of the following?

a. Large loans

b. Soldiers and guns

c. Ships and officers

d. All of the above

ANSWERS: 1. b; 2. d; 3. c; 4. a; 5. d

Final Crusades

On October 19, 1781, British General Lord Cornwallis surrendered to George Washington at the Battle of Yorktown. The decisive victory for the Americans ended the revolution. During the battle, 8,000 French soldiers and a French navy fleet fought on the side of the Americans. There is no question that the American ambassador to France,

Benjamin Franklin, had used his powers of persuasion in convincing the French to fight on the side of the Americans. "This is really a generous nation, fond of glory, and particularly that of protecting the oppressed," Franklin wrote of France.[68]

Although hostilities had ended, Franklin remained in France for another four years. His main mission was to help negotiate a peace treaty with England, signed in 1783, but he found many other ways to stay busy at his borrowed estate in Passy. In 1784, he was called on to participate in a scientific study of what was known as "animal magnetism."

During the 1770s, Austrian physician Franz Friedrich Anton Mesmer arrived in Paris, proclaiming that he had found a new way to treat virtually every known disease. According to Mesmer, a magnetic fluid flowed through each person's body, and every human disease and infirmity was caused by an imbalance of this fluid. Mesmer claimed to be able to restore balance to this fluid, either by manipulating the patient's body with his hands or by use of a magnetized iron wand. Mesmer said his technique, which was also known as "mesmerism," could not only cure disease but also blindness, deafness, and other handicaps.

For years, Mesmer was the talk of French society. Among his followers were French queen Marie Antoinette, military leader Marquis de Lafayette, and Franklin's grandson, Temple. Demonstrations of animal magnetism often featured groups of patients—sitting cross-legged in circles, linked arm in arm—while Mesmer or an assistant poked them with a metal wand, supposedly releasing a flow of magnetic energy. Once the treatment started, the patients often carried on in shrieks and laughter as they felt the magnetism coursing through their bodies.

Hundreds of patients flocked to Mesmer, hoping he could cure their ills. King Louis XVI was dubious of Mesmer's claims and asked the French Academy of Sciences to investigate animal magnetism. Franklin agreed to serve on a commission impaneled to look into mesmerism.

Because Franklin was suffering through a painful attack of gout and was unable to leave his estate in Passy, much of the commission's work was performed at Franklin's home. In fact, Mesmer's associate, Charles Deslon, tried several times to magnetize Franklin by prodding him with an iron wand, but the treatments had no effect on Franklin's aching feet.

Other experiments conducted in the presence of commission members also indicated that animal magnetism was a fraud. Franklin agreed with the commission's findings and placed his name on the report that exposed the truth about mesmerism. He told his grandson that he should not feel ashamed that he was fooled into believing the validity of animal magnetism. People are always looking for miracles, he told Temple, "and deceptions as absurd [as mesmerism] have supported themselves for ages."[69]

RETURN TO PHILADELPHIA

As Franklin spent his final months in Passy, he gave considerable thought to remaining in France for the rest of his life. He loved the French people and they truly loved him. At the age of 79, he continued to suffer from gout and was also afflicted with kidney stones. He wondered if he could survive the ocean voyage home. He had submitted his resignation as French ambassador to Congress, but hoped that Temple would be asked to stay on in Paris as a diplomat for the American government. When Temple was not offered the position, Franklin decided to return home.

The Franklins departed Passy on July 12, 1785. Louis XVI sent Benjamin Franklin a gift—a portrait of the king surrounded by 408 diamonds. Queen Marie Antoinette sent her carriage and team of mules to carry Franklin and his grandsons to the port of Le Havre on the French coast of the English Channel. On the day the Franklins left Passy, Benny Bache described in his diary his grandfather's somber mood: "A mournful silence reigned around him, broken only by a few sobs." [70]

Franklin's spirits brightened when he stepped off the ship in Philadelphia that September. The Franklins were greeted by a huge crowd that cheered wildly as the former ambassador made his way down the gangplank. Bells rang in churches and cannons boomed in salute. His daughter, Sally, embraced Franklin, welcoming him home for the final time. Sally's family, the Baches, had moved into Franklin's house in Philadelphia, and Franklin planned to make his home with them.

Franklin soon settled into life back in Philadelphia, but by no means did he intend to pursue a quiet, uneventful retirement. He planned to finish his autobiography. By now, the country had won its independence, and Franklin would take part in the deliberations over the new Constitution. The new administrators of the American government would soon carve a capital city out of marshland donated by the states of Maryland and Virginia. It would come to be known as the District of Columbia, so named to honor Christopher Columbus, the discover of the New World. Following the death of George Washington, Congress voted to name the city Washington, D.C.

In Franklin's mind, however, there was still one nagging issue that had been left unresolved by the revolution and the drafting of the Constitution. When the Continental Congress deliberated over the terms of the Declaration of Independence, a statement accusing King George of encouraging slavery was stricken from the document, out of fear that the representatives of the Southern colonies would reject the document. During the Constitutional Convention, Franklin had a hand in forging the "Great Compromise," which determined that each state would send two senators to the Senate while representation in the House would be based on population. The compromise also included the "three-fifths" clause—stating that each slave would be counted as three-fifths of a person when calculating the population of a state for representation in the House—a measure designed to ensure that the thinly-populated Southern states maintained an influential voice in the government.

Franklin had long felt that compromise was a necessary part of democracy, but following the Constitutional Convention, he found himself unwilling to accept any compromise that permitted slavery to endure in American society. Slavery was an important component of the economy of the South: the labor provided by thousands of slaves was considered vital for the operation of the enormous plantations. Indeed, in the years to come, slavery would become even more important to the South. Following Eli Whitney's invention of the cotton gin in 1793, the process of cleaning the seeds and impurities from cotton was greatly speeded up, making it economically feasible to grow cotton. The market for American-grown cotton exploded in Europe, making it the most important crop produced in the South. The importation of slaves from Africa and the West Indies continued, leading to the growth of the abolitionist movement in America during the 1800s. Bitter relations between the North and the South eventually culminated in the Civil War (1861–1865).

ABOLITIONIST

Franklin had long felt slavery was wrong, even though

Benjamin Franklin's Birthday

Benjamin Franklin was born on January 6, 1706, but today his birth date is regarded as January 17, 1706. Why is his date of birth celebrated 11 days after the day on which he was really born? The answer can be found in a change in the calendar that occurred in 1752.

Until then, England used what was known as the Julian calendar—the calendar first employed by Julius Caesar in the year 45 B.C. The Julian calendar fixed the year at 365 days and added an extra day every fourth, or leap, year—a system that is still employed today.

But the Julian calendar was not perfect. It was based on an average of 365.25 days per year, which is 11 minutes and 15 seconds longer than the true length of the year. At first, such a brief discrepancy was hardly noticeable, but over the centuries important holidays as well as the beginnings of the seasons started falling on incorrect days. In fact, the calendar added a full day for more than 30 years he owned slaves and employed them in his Philadelphia household and often accepted advertisements for slave sales for the pages of the *Gazette*. He took a slave named Peter to England on his first diplomatic mission to London in 1757. In fact,

every 128 years. By 1752, the Julian calendar was 11 days ahead.

England adopted a calendar commissioned by Pope Gregory XIII in 1582, which eliminated the extra days. The so-called Gregorian calendar also compensated for each year's extra 11 minutes and 15 seconds by eliminating leap years that occur in century years that are not divisible by 400. It means that the years 1600 and 2000 were leap years, but the years 1700, 1800 and 1900 were not.

When England adopted the Gregorian calendar, 11 days were eliminated. Therefore, everybody born in England or in an English colony prior to 1752 had new birthdays that were 11 days later than their original birthdays. Another of America's founding fathers who found himself with a new birthday was George Washington, who was really born on February 11, 1731. Today Washington's birthday is celebrated on February 22.

when he returned to Philadelphia from France and moved in with his daughter and her husband, Richard Bache, he discovered a slave named Bob living in the home's slave quarters.

For years, though, Franklin had published pamphlets denouncing slavery as well as the harsh treatment of the people in bondage. Franklin, always a believer in the fruits of hard work, believed that slavery would make whites lazy. He wrote,

> The Whites who have Slaves, not labouring, are enfeebled, and therefore not so generally prolific; the Slaves being worked too hard, and ill-fed, their Constitutions are broken, and the Deaths among them are more than the Births, so that a continual Supply is needed from Africa.[71]

In America, the abolitionist movement started as early as the 1750s. Most of the early abolitionists were Quaker merchants, who refused to employ slave labor. Quakers also offered to educate the children of slaves in their schools, a notion that was vehemently rejected by most other segments of society. Although he was not a Quaker, Franklin agreed with the idea of educating the children of slaves and, in 1758, he responded to a request made by an English charitable group to help start a school in Philadelphia for the children of slaves. Deborah and Benjamin Franklin sent their young household slave Othello to the school as one of the institution's first pupils. Later, Franklin helped start similar schools in Virginia, New York, and Rhode Island. While traveling as colonial postmaster, Franklin often made a point of visiting the schools. Watching the young children absorb their lessons, Franklin wrote that he held "a higher Opinion of the Natural Capacities of the black Race, than I have ever before entertained. Their Apprehension [is] quick, their Memory as Strong, and their Docility in every Respect equal to that of the White Children."[72]

As he settled into retirement in Philadelphia, Franklin resolved to pursue the abolition of slavery as his final crusade. In 1787, Franklin accepted the presidency of the Pennsylvania Society for the Abolition of Slavery, the first abolitionist group in America. In 1790, Franklin presented a petition to Congress calling for a law to end slavery. The petition was denounced by Southern lawmakers and quickly rejected.

Following the rejection of his petition, Franklin decided to pursue his goal the same way he had often organized crusades throughout his life—by using the power of the written word to demand change. In March 1790, he anonymously published an essay in a local newspaper titled "Sidi Mehemet Ibrahim on the Slave Trade." The essay purportedly gave the opinions of an Algerian political leader responding to the criticism of abolitionists who opposed the enslavement of white Europeans for work on the Algerian farms. "If we forbear to make slaves of their people, who in this climate are to cultivate our lands?" asked Sidi. "Who are to perform the common labors of our city, and in our families?"[73]

The purpose of the essay was to show that the arguments made by the Algerian were as hollow as the arguments made by the Southern lawmakers, who had rejected his petition just weeks before. During the debate in the House, Georgia Congressman James Jackson denounced Franklin's petition, claiming that slavery was sanctioned in the Bible. Likewise, Franklin, in the guise of the Algerian, made an equally ridiculous claim, asserting that slavery was sanctioned by the Koran, the holy book of Islam. Said Franklin's essay, "Let us then hear no more of this detestable proposition, the [freedom] of Christian slaves, the adoption of which would, by depreciating our lands and houses, and thereby depriving so many good citizens of their properties, create universal discontent, and provoke insurrections."[74]

FINAL DAYS

Franklin's final act of public service was to help Secretary of State Thomas Jefferson settle a dispute with England over a territorial boundary with Canada. While he was still active, Franklin suffered from many troubling ailments, including painful attacks from gout as well as kidney stones.

Throughout his life, Franklin had displayed a tremendous tolerance for other faiths. He made a habit of donating money to all religious organizations in Philadelphia, helping them erect their places of worship. In fact, a new synagogue erected in Philadelphia in 1788 was built with the help of a donation from Franklin. In 1790, Franklin wrote a letter to Reverend Ezra Stiles, the president of Yale University, in which he responded to Stiles's questions about his religious faith. Franklin—who as a young boy was headed to the ministry—acknowledged to Stiles that he believed in "one God, Creator of the Universe" [75] and that he found the system of morals practiced by Christians as "the best the world ever saw or is likely to see." [76] He admitted to Stiles, though, that he harbored doubts about the divinity of Christ. Expecting to live no more than a few more months, Franklin told Stiles that he saw no use in pondering the question at this point in his life, because soon he expected to have "the opportunity of knowing the truth with less trouble." [77]

Early in April 1790, Dr. John Jones was called to the Franklin home. He found the elder Franklin quite ill, particularly from the pain brought on by his kidney stones. Later, the doctor wrote:

> He was seized with a feverish indisposition, without any particular symptoms attending it, till the third or fourth day, when he complained of a pain in the left breast, which increased till it became extremely acute, attended with a cough and laborious breathing. During this state when the severity of his pain drew forth a groan of complaint, he . . . acknowledged his grateful sense of the many blessings he had received from that Supreme Being, who had

After a long life of innovation and achievement, Benjamin Franklin was laid to rest in the graveyard at Christ Church in Philadelphia, Pennsylvania. Millions of visitors each year pay their respects to this great inventor, writer, and statesman.

raised him from small and low beginnings to such high rank and consideration among men . . . and made no doubt but his present afflictions were kindly intended to wean him from a world, in which he was no longer fit to act the part assigned him. In this frame of body and mind he continued . . . when his pain and difficulty of breathing entirely left him, and his family were flattering themselves with the hopes of his recovery, when [a swelling], which had formed itself in his lungs, suddenly burst, and discharged a great quantity of matter, which he continued to throw up while he had sufficient strength to do it; but as that failed, the organs of respiration became gradually oppressed, a calm lethargic state succeeded, and on the 17th of April 1790, about eleven o'clock at night, he quietly expired, closing a long and useful life of eighty-four years and three months.[78]

Franklin was buried next to his wife Deborah and the couple's young son, Franky, in the cemetery at Christ Church in Philadelphia. More than 20,000 people lined Market Street as the funeral procession made its way from the Franklin home to the church-yard. At the time, it was the largest gathering of people in the history of America.

Test Your Knowledge

I What was Franklin's main mission in remaining in France after the end of the Revolutionary War?

　a. To expose mesmerism as a fraud

　b. To help negotiate a peace treaty between France and England

　c. To seek a cure for his gout

　d. To study new advances in the printing industry

2 How was Franklin received upon his final return to Philadelphia in 1785?

　a. A small official party greeted him at the docks when his ship landed.

　b. Only his daughter, Sally, greeted him as he stepped off the ship.

　c. He was met by cheering crowds, ringing church bells, and cannon salutes.

　d. He was arrested as a traitor as soon as he stepped onto American soil.

3 What was the "Great Compromise"?

　a. A system by which each state would send two legislators to the Senate, but representation in the House would be determined by a state's population

　b. A system designed to end slavery in the Southern states

　c. A system of creating an Electoral College to determine the selection of a president

　d. None of the above

4 What was Franklin's final crusade?

a. Abolition of slavery in America

b. Creation of a federal banking system

c. Establishment of the National Science Academy

d. None of the above

5 What were Franklin's feelings about religious faith
and spirituality?

a. Franklin tolerated and respected all faiths,
frequently donating money to religious institutions,
including churches and synagogues.

b. Franklin believed in "One God, Creator of the
Universe."

c. Franklin had doubts about the divinity of Christ.

d. All of the above.

ANSWERS: 1. b; 2. c; 3. a; 4. a; 5. d

Following in the Footsteps of Franklin

During his lifetime, Benjamin Franklin lived in four cities—Boston and Philadelphia in America, and London and Paris in Europe. Each city has found ways to honor Franklin's memory, as well as his achievements in science, politics, and education. But the honors bestowed on Franklin do not end there. Throughout America, dozens of communities have found ways to honor Franklin, adopting his name for schools, community centers, streets, parks, bridges, towns, and counties. Indeed, 15 counties in America that are named "Franklin" selected their name to honor Benjamin Franklin.

There was briefly a state named "Franklin" as well. In 1784, the counties of Washington, Sullivan, and Greene in western North Carolina were granted autonomy by the state government in order to form their own state. The three counties formed the state of Franklin, named in honor of America's ambassador, who was still living in France. A state constitution was written and the town of Greeneville was designated as the state capital, but political leaders balked at joining the United States. Attacks by hostile Native Americans soon convinced the settlers that they could not maintain their autonomy, and, in 1790, the state of Franklin was dissolved. Eventually, the three counties became part of Tennessee.

Elsewhere, the Franklin Mountains in Texas are named in honor of Benjamin Franklin—but Franklin County, Texas, is not. That county was named after Benjamin Cromwell Franklin, a nineteenth-century judge. The judge did, however, attend Franklin College

So popular and well known is the image of Benjamin Franklin, that visitors to Philadelphia can still find themselves greeted by a Franklin look-alike as they tour historic sites such as Elfreth's Alley.

in Athens, Georgia, which *was* named in honor of Benjamin Franklin

One place named in honor of Franklin is not even on this planet. Astronomers named the Franklin crater on the moon in honor of the great scientist of the eighteenth century. The 90-mile-wide circular crater is in the northeast corner of the full moon as it is visible from Earth. Franklin is an impact crater, meaning it was created by an object, probably a meteor, smashing into the moon millions of years ago.

VISITING BOSTON AND PHILADELPHIA

Visitors to Boston hoping to trace Franklin's footsteps as a young boy will find few places that have been preserved in the nearly three centuries since he left the city. For example, Franklin's birthplace on Milk Street and his second boyhood home on Hanover Street were razed long ago, although a plaque and bust of Franklin mark the Milk Street site as his birthplace. Visitors to the Hanover Street site will find it has been replaced by a Holocaust memorial to remember the victims of the Nazi atrocities during World War II. A government building stands on the site of Boston Latin School, where Franklin spent a year as a student, although a statue of Franklin has been placed out front. James Franklin's print shop on Queen Street, where Benjamin learned the printer's trade, is now a shelter for homeless people.

Although Franklin left Boston as a teenager, he made provisions in his will to give something back to the city of his birth (as well as the city of Philadelphia and the states of Massachusetts and Pennsylvania). Franklin, of course, had only two years of formal education; most of his schooling was accomplished as a trade apprentice. As such, Franklin had the greatest respect for vocational education. In his will, he left money to Boston that was eventually used to establish a vocational school.

It took more than a century for the school to open due to delays caused by lengthy lawsuits brought against the city by Franklin's heirs, who contested the use of the money. Nevertheless, on September 25, 1908, what is known today as the Benjamin Franklin Institute of Technology opened its doors to 533 students. Since then, more than 85,000 young people have been educated in a variety of trades, including computer technology, construction, and automotive fields.

While traces of Franklin's life can still be found in

Boston, there is no question that Philadelphia has taken far more substantial steps to honor the man who was arguably the city's most famous and influential citizen. Franklin's original home in a court behind Market Street, built between 1763 and 1765, no longer exists. Franklin was serving as a diplomat in England at that time, so his wife Deborah supervised construction. By the time Franklin returned home from France many years later, Deborah had died and the house was occupied by the couple's daughter, Sally, her husband, Richard Bache, and their children. Arriving back in Philadelphia to find a home filled with grandchildren, Franklin, at the age of 81, decided to build an addition that would include a library and guest rooms. "I hardly know how to justify building a Library at an age that will so soon oblige me to quit it," he wrote, "but we are apt to forget that we are grown old, and Building is an amusement."[79]

Following Franklin's death, his heirs continued to reside in the home, then leased it to tenants. It was torn down in 1812 to make way for commercial development. Today, the site of the former home is part of Independence National Park, which also includes nearby Independence Hall and the Liberty Bell. Known as "Franklin Court," the site has been cleared and a 54-foot-high steel skeleton "ghost" structure showns visitors the architectural shape of the home.

Archaeologists have been working beneath the former home since the 1970s and have unearthed some 30,000 relics, many of which date back to Franklin's lifetime. Some of the relics are on display in a museum established by the National Park Service. Visitors can also see reproductions of Franklin's glass armonica, the swim fins he invented, and a Franklin stove.

Adjacent to Franklin Court are row houses at 316 and 318 Market Street that Franklin built in 1786 and 1787 with the idea of leasing them to tenants. Over the years, Franklin's heirs enlarged and renovated the buildings, although some of the original walls were incorporated into the larger structures. The houses passed out of the Franklin family's hands in 1914, but in 1954 they were acquired by the National Park Service, which has taken steps to preserve them. Visitors to the house at 318 Market Street will find markings on the walls where some of the original features, such as fireplaces, were built.

The complex of buildings on the 300 block of Market Street includes the Franklin Post Office, which is the only post office in the United States that does not

Craven Street's Gruesome Past

When workers started renovating Benjamin Franklin's London residence at 36 Craven Street, they uncovered a gruesome discovery: human bones. Work had commenced on the house in 1997 to turn it into a museum celebrating Franklin's two trips to England as a diplomat representing the colonies. The bones were found by workers digging up the basement. In fact, construction workers unearthed some 1,500 bones, both human and animal.

The Craven Street home had been owned by the widow Margaret Stevenson. During Franklin's stay, English physician William Hewson also used the residence as a school to teach anatomy. Hewson married Margaret's daughter, Polly.

Hewson is given credit for many advances in medical science, including the use of dead bodies to teach anatomy to students. Today the dissection of bodies is a routine part of training for future doctors, but in Hewson's day it was considered unseemly for the bodies of the dead to be dissected—even by students who would gain a much better understanding of anatomy and,

fly the American flag—it did not yet exist when Franklin was appointed postmaster in 1775. Employees of the post office also stamp mail by hand, the way

therefore, be able to save lives with the knowledge they learned through the procedures.

Hewson had to resort to hiring grave robbers to steal corpses. Certainly, the type of people Hewson hired were not reputable members of London society. The crime of grave robbing was punishable by flogging and even death. As such, Hewson had to be careful about his activities. No doubt, he felt it was necessary to bury the dissected bodies in the basement.

Historians believe Franklin knew what was going on at the Craven Street house and most likely approved. He was, after all, a man of science. Hilaire Dubourcq, a spokesman for the Friends of the Benjamin Franklin House, the group sponsoring the renovation, told *People* magazine, "Whether Franklin knew what Hewson was doing—probably. But it was very doubtful that he participated."

As for Dr. Hewson, he faced an unfortunate death. In 1774, while conducting a dissection, he accidentally cut himself. The cut became infected and Hewson died of blood poisoning.

Franklin and his employees applied postmarks more than two centuries ago. Also on the block is a museum of printing, which demonstrates the techniques Franklin used to produce his newspaper and other publications, as well as the restored office of *The Aurora and General Advertiser*, a newspaper published by Franklin's grandson, Benjamin Franklin Bache.

Nearby, the Christ Church cemetery has been preserved and visitors can peer through the fence to view the gravesites of Benjamin and Deborah. Independence Hall, where the Declaration of Independence was debated and signed, is open to public tours. Visitors may also tour Carpenter's Hall, first home of the Library Company and the American Philosophical Society. The Fireman's Hall Museum, established to celebrate the history of firefighting in Philadelphia, pays tribute to Franklin as well.

LONDON AND PARIS

In England, a museum of Franklin's life in London has been established at 36 Craven Street, the home he shared with Margaret Stevenson and her daughter, Polly, on his first mission to London. For years, the Craven Street property languished, featuring no more

Through his many contributions, Benjamin Franklin has earned an honored place in America's history. This 20-foot-high statue, sculpted by James Earle Fraser, is part of the Benjamin Franklin National Memorial at Philadelphia's Franklin Institute, a museum devoted to scientific discovery and exploration.

than a plaque marking the fact that Franklin had resided there. The home suffered damage when it was bombed during World War II, then was patched up and served as commercial space for the next three decades.

Franklin's second home in London at 7 Craven Street was demolished years ago.

In the 1970s, the Friends of the Benjamin Franklin House organized to renovate 36 Craven Street and turn it into a museum of Franklin's two missions to England. It took several years for the organization to raise the $3.5 million needed for the restoration, but work finally commenced in the 1990s. The workers have returned the home to the condition in which it existed when Franklin lived there. "It's pretty amazing that this house, which is 200-plus years old, is still around," Marcia Balisciano, director of the Benjamin Franklin House, told a reporter. "We have a major opportunity to create something out of nothing with it."[80]

What makes the house in London truly special is that it is the only one of Franklin's residences that still exists—his homes in Boston, Philadelphia, and Paris disappeared years ago. In fact, the village of Passy, where Franklin lived while serving as ambassador, no longer exists—it was absorbed by the city of Paris in 1859.

While serving in France, Franklin spent ten years living at the grand estate of Jacques-Donatien Leray de

Chaumont, a wealthy merchant who wholeheartedly supported the American Revolution. The de Chaumont estate has since been torn down, replaced by modern apartment buildings. Nevertheless, at the corner of Rue Raynourd and Rue Singer in Paris, the former location of the estate, visitors will find a plaque featuring a portrait of Franklin commemorating the ambassador's residence at the location. The city has also named a street, Rue Benjamin Franklin, in memory of the American ambassador.

Nearby, a statue of Franklin has been erected in a city park. The statue was presented as a gift to the French government in 1905 by John H. Harjes, a banker from Philadelphia who lived in Paris. The engraving on the base of the statue reads:

Benjamin Franklin, 1706–1790, the genius who freed America and flooded Europe with light: the sage whom two worlds call their own.[81]

Test Your Knowledge

I In which of the following cities did Benjamin Franklin NOT live?

a. London

b. Philadelphia

c. Boston

d. Madrid

2 The short-lived state of Franklin (once part of North Carolina) is now part of what state?

a. Tennessee

b. Kentucky

c. South Carolina

d. None of the above

3 What is the "ghost" of Franklin Court?

a. A legend that the spirit of Franklin still haunts his home in Philadelphia

b. A structure on the site of Franklin's former residence showing the outline or "skeleton" of the house that once stood there

c. An eerie artifact found at Franklin's former home in Philadelphia

d. None of the above

4 In what year did the National Park Service acquire the houses that Franklin had built on Market Street?
   a. 1954
   b. 1960
   c. 1976
   d. 2001

5 What is special about Franklin's residence in London?
   a. It is where Franklin is buried
   b. It is the place where Franklin first experimented with electricity
   c. It is the only one of Franklin's former homes still standing
   d. None of the above

ANSWERS: 1. d; 2. a; 3. b; 4. a; 5. c

1706 Benjamin Franklin is born in Boston on January 17.

1718 Apprenticed to his brother James.

1722 Writes "Silence Dogood" essays.

1723 Makes his way to Philadelphia and finds employment as a printer.

1724 Sails to London to buy a printing press; learns his sponsor is penniless and is forced to find work as a printer.

1726 Returns to Philadelphia as a shopkeeper.

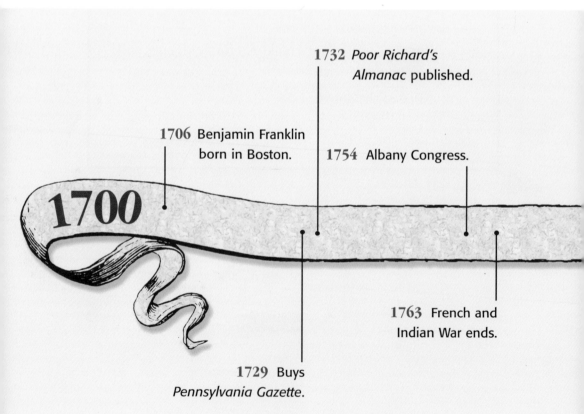

1732 *Poor Richard's Almanac* published.

1706 Benjamin Franklin born in Boston.

1754 Albany Congress.

1700

1763 French and Indian War ends.

1729 Buys *Pennsylvania Gazette.*

1728 Forms a partnership with Hugh Meredith to start a printing business.

1729 Buys the *Pennsylvania Gazette*.

1730 Enters a common law marriage with Deborah Read Rogers.

1731 Is instrumental in founding the Library Company of Philadelphia.

1732 Publishes first edition of *Poor Richard's Almanac*.

1736 Four-year-old Francis Folger Franklin dies of smallpox.

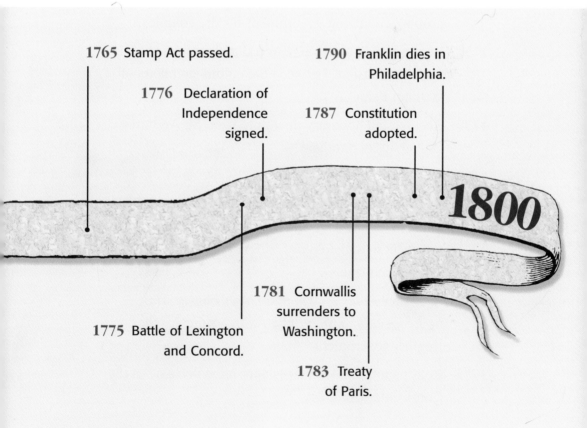

1765 Stamp Act passed.

1776 Declaration of Independence signed.

1790 Franklin dies in Philadelphia.

1787 Constitution adopted.

1800

1775 Battle of Lexington and Concord.

1781 Cornwallis surrenders to Washington.

1783 Treaty of Paris.

1737 Is appointed deputy postmaster for the colonies.

1741 Designs Franklin stove.

1743 Establishes American Philosophical Society.

1748 Retires from active participation in his printing business; devotes the rest of his life to scientific study and public service.

1749 Experiments with electricity and invents the battery and lightning rod.

1751 Is elected to Pennsylvania Assembly.

1752 Performs kite and key experiment.

1754 Publishes "Join or Die" cartoon in the *Gazette*; proposes common government for the colonies.

1757 Represents Pennsylvania as a diplomat in London; settles tax dispute between the colony and heirs of William Penn.

1759 Receives an honorary doctorate from St. Andrews University in Scotland.

1762 Sails home to Philadelphia.

1764 Returns to London to argue against the Stamp Tax; remains for the next eleven years as a diplomat representing the colonies as fervor builds in America for independence.

1773 Publishes *Rules by Which a Great Empire May be Reduced to a Small One*, which ridicules the English government.

1775 Returns to Philadelphia; is appointed delegate to the Continental Congress.

1776 Signs the Declaration of Independence; arrives in France as American ambassador.

1781 Cornwallis surrenders to Washington; Franklin is appointed to committee to negotiate peace treaty with England.

1785 Arrives home in Philadelphia.

1787 Serves as delegate to the Constitutional Convention; accepts presidency of the Pennsylvania Society for the Abolition of Slavery.

1790 Dies on April 17; 20,000 people attend his funeral.

Notes

CHAPTER 1
"Doctor" Benjamin Franklin

1. Walter Isaacson, *Benjamin Franklin: An American Life* (New York: Simon and Schuster, 2003), 351.
2. Ibid., 319.
3. Ibid., 319.
4. Ibid., 264.
5. Ibid., 265.
6. "Benjamin Franklin: Inquiring Mind," www.pbs.org/benfranklin/ 13_inquiring_medical.html.
7. N.J.C. Andreasen, "Benjamin Franklin: Physicus et Medicus," *Journal of the American Medical Association*, no. 1, vol. 236, July 5, 1976, 61.
8. Isaacson, *Benjamin Franklin: An American Life*, 243.
9. Ibid., 83.
10. Ibid., 83.
11. Ibid., 319.

CHAPTER 2
Student and Apprentice

12. Isaacson, *Benjamin Franklin: An American Life*, 16.
13. Albert Henry Smyth, *The Writings of Benjamin Franklin, Volume V* (London: The MacMillan Company, 1906), 543.
14. Benjamin Franklin, *The Autobiography of Benjamin Franklin*. (Boston: Bedford/ St. Martin's, 1993), 33.

15. Carl Van Doren, *Benjamin Franklin*. (New York: Book-of-the-Month Club, 1980), 144.
16. Clifford A. Pickover, *The Zen of Magic Squares, Circles, and Stars*. (Princeton, N.J.: Princeton University Press, 2002), 155.
17. Van Doren, *Benjamin Franklin*, 145–146.
18. Isaacson, *Benjamin Franklin: An American Life*, 28–29.
19. Ibid., 26.
20. Ibid., 27.
21. Ibid., 27.
22. Ibid., 28.
23. Gordon S. Wood, *The Americanization of Benjamin Franklin*. (New York: Penguin Press, 2004), 21.
24. Catherine Drinker Bowen, *The Most Dangerous Man in America: Scenes from the Life of Benjamin Franklin*. (Boston: Little, Brown and Co., 1974), 24.
25. Ibid., 25.
26. Ibid., 23–24.
27. Ibid., 33.

CHAPTER 3
Printer and Journalist

28. Isaacson, *Benjamin Franklin: An American Life*, 64.
29. Ibid., 75.
30. Ibid., 69.
31. Van Doren, *Benjamin Franklin*, 100.
32. Franklin, *The Autobiography of Benjamin Franklin,* 100.

33. Isaacson, *Benjamin Franklin: An American Life*, 99.
34. Ibid., 98.

CHAPTER 4
The Search for Useful Knowledge
35. Verner W. Crane, *Benjamin Franklin and a Rising People.* (Boston: Little, Brown and Co., 1954), 38.
36. Van Doren, *Benjamin Franklin*, 434.
37. Isaacson, *Benjamin Franklin: An American Life*, 132.
38. Ibid., 134.
39. Ibid., 136.
40. Ibid., 137.
41. Franklin, *The Autobiography of Benjamin Franklin,* 146.
42. Isaacson, *Benjamin Franklin: An American Life*, 426.
43. W. Thomas Marrocco, "The String Quartet Attributed to Benjamin Franklin," *Proceedings of the American Philosophical Society*, vol. 116, no. 6, Dec. 21, 1972, 480.
44. Willard Sterne Randall, *A Little Revenge: Benjamin Franklin and His Son.* (Boston: Little, Brown and Co., 1984), 161–162.

CHAPTER 5
Community Organizer
45. Isaacson, *Benjamin Franklin: An American Life*, 105.
46. Ibid., 104.

47. Ibid., 105.
48. Ibid., 104.
49. Van Doren, *Benjamin Franklin*, 131.
50. Isaacson, *Benjamin Franklin: An American Life*, 153–154.
51. Ibid., 146.
52. "Penn in the 18th Century," University of Pennsylvania, www.archives.upenn.edu/histy/features/1700s/penn1700s.html.
53. Van Doren, *Benjamin Franklin*, 139.
54. "American Philosophical Society," Franklin's Philadelphia, www.ushistory.org/franklin/philadelphia/aps.htm.
55. Isaacson, *Benjamin Franklin: An American Life*, 159.
56. Ibid., 160.

CHAPTER 6
Diplomat and Patriot
57. Isaacson, *Benjamin Franklin: An American Life*, 311.
58. Ibid., 313.
59. Ibid., 313.
60. Van Doren, *Benjamin Franklin*, 553.
61. Isaacson, *Benjamin Franklin: An American Life*, 458–459.
62. Isaacson, *Benjamin Franklin: An American Life*, 222–223.
63. "Benjamin Franklin," American Revolution Homepage, www.americanrevwar.homestead.com/files/FRANKLIN.HTM.

64. Isaacson, *Benjamin Franklin: An American Life*, 282.
65. Ibid., 420.
66. Ibid., 421.
67. Ibid., 421.

CHAPTER 7
Final Crusades

68. Isaacson, *Benjamin Franklin: An American Life*, 393.
69. Ibid., 427.
70. Ibid., 433.
71. Claude-Anne Lopez and Eugenia W. Herbert, *The Private Franklin: The Man and His Family* (New York: W.W. Norton and Co., 1975), 294.
72. Ibid., 296.
73. Isaacson, *Benjamin Franklin: An American Life*, 466.
74. Ibid., 467.
75. "Benjamin Franklin on His Religious Faith," *American Heritage*, vol. 7, no. 1, December 1955, 105.

76. Ibid.
77. Ibid.
78. William Pepper, *The Medical Side of Benjamin Franklin* (Philadelphia: William J. Campbell, 1911), 116–117.

CHAPTER 8
Following in the Footsteps of Franklin

79. "Franklin Court," National Park Service, www.nps.gov/inde/franklin-court.html.
80. Andrea Gerlin, "Makeover for Ben Franklin's London Home," *Philadelphia Inquirer*, Oct. 8, 2003, E-1.
81. Daniel Jouve, *Paris: Birthplace of the USA* (Paris: Grund, 1995), 91.

Andreasen, N.J.C. "Benjamin Franklin: Physicus et Medicus." *Journal of the American Medical Association* Vol. 236, No. 1, July 5, 1976.

Bowen, Catherine Drinker. *The Most Dangerous Man in America: Scenes from the Life of Benjamin Franklin*. Boston, MA: Little, Brown and Co., 1974.

Crane, Verner W. *Benjamin Franklin and a Rising People*. Boston, MA: Little, Brown and Co., 1954.

Fleming, Candace. *Ben Franklin's Almanac*. New York, NY: Atheneum Books, 2003.

Franklin, Benjamin. *The Autobiography of Benjamin Franklin*. Boston, MA: Bedford/St. Martin's, 1993.

Isaacson, Walter. *Benjamin Franklin: An American Life*. New York, NY: Simon & Schuster, 2003.

Lopez, Claude-Anne, and Eugenia W. Herbert. *The Private Franklin: The Man and His Family*. New York, NY: W.W. Norton and Co., 1975.

"Out of the Past: Cellar Dwellers. Workers Get a Ghoulish Surprise in Ben Franklin's London Basement." *People*, April 6, 1998.

Pepper, William. *The Medical Side of Benjamin Franklin*. Philadelphia, PA: William J. Campbell, 1911.

Randall, Willard Sterne. *A Little Revenge: Benjamin Franklin and His Son*. Boston, MA: Little, Brown and Co., 1984.

Smyth, Albert Henry. *The Writings of Benjamin Franklin, Volume V*. London, UK: The MacMillan Company, 1906.

Wilcox, William B., ed. *The Papers of Benjamin Franklin*. New Haven, CT: Yale University Press, 1972.

Wood, Gordon S. *The Americanization of Benjamin Franklin*. New York, NY: Penguin Press, 2004.

Ashby, Ruth. *The Amazing Mr. Franklin, or, The Boy Who Read Everything*. Atlanta, GA: Peachtree Publications Ltd., 2004.

The Ben Franklin Book of Easy and Incredible Experiments: A Franklin Institute Science Museum Book. Hoboken, NJ: Wiley, 1995.

Fish, Bruce. *Benjamin Franklin: American Statesman, Scientist, and Writer*. Philadelphia, PA: Chelsea House, 2000.

Fradin, Dennis B. *The Signers: The Fifty-six Stories Behind the Declaration of Independence*. New York, NY: Walker & Co., 2002.

Fradin, Dennis B. *Who Was Ben Franklin?* New York, NY: Grosset & Dunlap, 2002.

Murphy, Frank. *Ben Franklin and the Magic Squares*. New York, NY: Random House, 2001.

Roop, Peter. *Benjamin Franklin*. New York, NY: Scholastic Reference, 2001.

WEBSITES

American Philosophical Society
www.amphilsoc.org

American Revolution Homepage
www.americanrevwar.homestead.com

Benjamin Franklin Institute of Technology
www.bfit.edu

Franklin Institute
http://sln.fi.edu

The Friends of Franklin, Inc.
www.benfranklin2006.org

HAL MARCOVITZ was born and raised in Benjamin Franklin's hometown of Philadelphia. He now lives in Chalfont, Pennsylvania, with his wife, Gail, and daughters Ashley and Michelle. He works as a journalist and is the author of more than 70 books for young readers as well as the satirical novel *Painting the White House*.

Special thanks to Irene D. Coffey and Virginia Ward of the Franklin Institute for their assistance in this project.